THE COLLECTS
OF
THOMAS CRANMER

THE COLLECTS
OF
THOMAS CRANMER

Compiled and Presented
for Devotional Use
by

C. Frederick Barbee and Paul F. M. Zahl

WILLIAM B. EERDMANS PUBLISHING COMPANY
GRAND RAPIDS, MICHIGAN / CAMBRIDGE, U.K.

© 1999 Wm. B. Eerdmans Publishing Co.
255 Jefferson Ave. S.E., Grand Rapids, Michigan 49503 /
P.O. Box 163, Cambridge CB3 9PU U.K.

Printed in the United States of America

04 03 02 01 00   7 6 5 4 3

Library of Congress Cataloging-in-Publication Data

Church of England.
[Book of common prayer. Collects]
The collects of Thomas Cranmer / compiled and presented for
devotional use by C. Frederick Barbee and Paul F. M. Zahl.
p.   cm.
Includes bibliographical references.
ISBN 0-8028-3845-6 (cloth : alk. paper)
1. Church of England. Book of common prayer.
Collects.   2. Church of England — Liturgy — Meditations.
3. Collects — Meditations.   I. Cranmer, Thomas, 1489-1556.
II. Barbee, C. Frederick.   III. Zahl, Paul F. M.   IV. Title.
BX5145.A62   1999
264'.036 — dc21   98-44941
CIP

This book is dedicated
to
Edward L. Salmon, Jr.
XIII Bishop of South Carolina
Friend, Mentor, and Companion in Ministry

Contents

FOREWORD

The Collects of Thomas Cranmer

Episcopalians who are adults today have lived through a period of extraordinary liturgical change. In the brief span of thirty years, the four-hundred-year-old Prayer Book tradition has been largely swept away.

But what seems to us a turbulent time pales before what our English ecclesiastical ancestors experienced in the tumultuous years of the Reformation. From the medieval Latin Mass retained by Henry VIII, to the first Book of Common Prayer of 1549, to the second Prayer Book of Edward VI only three years later, to the return of the Roman liturgy under Queen Mary, to the restoration of the Book of Common Prayer by Queen Elizabeth — all of this transpired in ten years' time.

One constant that remained throughout, and still is with us in the contemporary liturgies of our day, is the Collect. Imagine being transported in a time machine to fifth-century Rome on a particular Sunday of the church year and knowing enough Latin to recognize with delight and surprise the very same prayer to be found for that day in the Book of Common Prayer!

That is entirely probable, for the vast majority of the Prayer Book Collects are in fact pre-Reformation. Most are taken from the Sacramentaries of three famous Bishops of Rome: Leo I (440-461), Gelasius (492-496), and Gregory the Great (590-604). A Sacramentary was a book that contained the fixed prayers of the Eucharist and the variable Collects of the day.

What is a Collect? The origin of the term *collecta*, while rather obscure, refers to the "gathering of the people together" as well as to the "collecting up" of the petitions of individual members of the congregation into one prayer. This at first extemporaneous prayer would later also be connected to the Epistle and Gospel appointed for the day. A Collect is a short prayer that asks "for one thing only" (Fortescue) and is peculiar to the liturgies of the Western Churches, being unknown in the Churches of the East. It is also a literary form (an art comparable to the sonnet) usually, but not always, consisting of five parts.

I. The Address

The invocation is to the Father. "And in that day ye shall ask me nothing . . . whatsoever ye shall ask the Father in my name, he will give it to you" (St. John 16:23). The exceptions to this rule are Advent III, Lent I, and St. Stephen's Day, when the Son is addressed directly. Trinity Sunday also stands outside this maxim, since in that case there is no distinction of Persons.

II. The Acknowledgment

This gives "the foundation of doctrine upon which our request is made" (Dean Goulburn). It reflects some quality of God related to that which we shall be asking Him in the Petition: His power, His grace, His transcendence, His mercy. In a few cases, however, what is acknowledged is our weakness or frailty or sinfulness.

III. The Petition

Here is the actual prayer concerning basic needs: cleansing, forgiveness, protection, guidance, comfort, holiness, love.

IV. The Aspiration

Not appearing in all Collects, this is introduced by the conjunction "that." An example is found in Trinity XXI: pardon and peace are desired *so that* we may be better fitted for God's service. The petition ("pardon and peace") is not an end in itself but claims a higher purpose in the aspiration.

V. *The Pleading*

". . . through Jesus Christ our Lord." Christ is our only mediator and advocate. Through Jesus alone can we draw near to the Father. The pleading historically contained the doxological words "who liveth and reigneth with thee and the Holy Ghost, ever one God, world without end." This ending was so well-known that Archbishop Cranmer either omitted it or placed "&c" in lieu of it. But this omission led to forgetting, and the full wording was restored to some Collects in 1662 and, finally, to all of them in the 1979 American edition.

Here is the pattern for the familiar and much-loved Collect for Purity from the service of Holy Communion:

    I. Almighty God,
   II. unto whom all hearts are open, all desires known, and from whom no secrets are hid,
  III. cleanse the thoughts of our hearts by the inspiration of thy Holy Spirit,
  IV. that we may perfectly love thee, and worthily magnify thy holy name,
   V. through Jesus Christ our Lord, Amen.

Another example is that of Trinity XIX:

    I. O God,
  II. forasmuch as without thee we are not able to please thee
  III. mercifully grant that thy Holy Spirit may in all things direct and rule our hearts,
  IV.
   V. through Jesus Christ our Lord.

The Collects are not only necessary to the liturgy, but also are part of the pastoral tradition of the Church. The Prayer Book Collects are a priceless part of English-speaking Christianity. They are also for the present use of everyday Christians in the trials and testings of life. This book is meant to be used devotionally with Bible in hand.

We have chosen the Collect as the basis for this volume on the occasion of the 450th anniversary of the Book of Common Prayer. As we await the next round of liturgical change, we pray that the revisers will have a deep appreciation of the integrity of both Holy Scripture and the Prayer Book tradition, unlocking our liturgical heritage for generations to come.

The Cathedral Church of the Advent   C. Frederick Barbee
Birmingham, Alabama   Paul F. M. Zahl

Introduction

Cranmer's genius was not on the order of Augustine, Luther, or Mozart. He did not have the wide-ranging and confident breadth and brilliance of the first two nor the incredible focus and depth of Mozart. Rather, his genius consisted of that rare and mysterious virtue, humility.

This humility was neither passive nor pusillanimous as his uncomprehending critics have falsely charged. Diarmaid MacCullough in his magisterial biography has shown the caution and conservative spirit that led him only gradually to the beliefs that were to manifest themselves in the English Prayer Book. Cranmer's astonishing blend of self-effacement and persistence in the service of faith accounts for the care and discipline which produced the single greatest combination of liturgical forms in the Church's history. This perduring contribution, which was not possible during the reign of Henry VIII, could only have been fulfilled under the sympathetic and royal authority of Edward VI.

Cranmer's consistent obedience to "duly constituted" royal authority ("It is not given to private citizens to amend what is amiss but to quietly suffer what they cannot change") was a frustration under Henry, whose theology was medieval Catholic and not that of the Reformers. However, Cranmer saw the principle of obedience to royal authority as firmly grounded in Scripture and in the history of Christendom since Constantine. This loyalty to the crown and his selfless service seemed to evoke a loyalty in kind from Henry. It was Henry who saved him from several exceedingly dangerous plots against his life. Cranmer was too reticent and unschooled in Machiavellian Tudor politics to defend himself effectively in the arena of raw power ego conflicts. He had even been rebuked by Henry for the excessive magnanimity he had shown to his enemies in the rapid power shifts of his age.

The humility that divested his ego of self-righteous concerns focused his passion in service to his Lord's Kingdom amid the ambiguities and vicissitudes of earthly kingdoms. Obedience to the former must, according to Scripture (Romans 13:1-7, Titus 3:1), be channeled in patience through the latter. This was the basis for Cranmer's obedience to royal authority, an obedience which sustained him through the frustrations of Henry's reign and released his incomparable creativity to produce, during the reign of Edward VI, the two Prayer Books as well as the Forty-Two Articles and the Book of Homilies. But it was, of course, this very obedience which caused him such excruciating agony under the Roman Catholic Queen, Mary, when his consistent policy of commitment to "the powers that be [which] are ordained of God" (Romans 13:1) blew up in his face. Queen Mary demanded that he not only submit (which he was willing to do even before imprisonment), but also to abjure and deny publicly all that he had accomplished and sincerely believed, something Henry had never demanded.

Cranmer had publicly fought and voted against Henry's notorious Six Articles Act. They enshrined in law the worst of unreformed medieval Catholicism. This was not the action of a sycophant any more than were his lonely and ardent pleas for the lives of Thomas More, Bishop Fisher, and Anne Boleyn. But when the Articles became law he saw it as his biblical duty to submit. Henry did not demand that he deny his beliefs, only that he submit to the law. Queen Elizabeth was later to announce her firm policy that she would "not build windows into a man's soul" (a policy that Professor Powel Mills Dawley claimed to be an essential principle of the Anglican Reformation).

The policy of Queen Mary and Cardinal Pole was not merely to require submission to the reestablishment of Roman Catholicism and to discard the Reformation Articles and Prayer Book, but to use Cranmer to blacken the name of the Reformation itself. The story of the last two years of Cranmer's life has been told by his contemporary John Foxe. After two and one half years' imprisonment, enduring constant interrogation over some thirty months, watching his friends burn, and being offered the hope of saving his life on the condition of recanting, he finally succumbed and signed an abject confession and recantation. Brought to public trial to read this document, he astonished the witnesses by repudiating his confession and affirming the faith we now see in his prayers and teachings.

He was quickly seized and brought to the stake where he was burned, but not before freeing his hand and putting it first in the flame, "this hand that offendeth" (which had signed the earlier recantation). Diarmaid MacCullough, in his appreciation of Cranmer's ordeal, makes the observation, "After the miserable history of brainwashing and interruption in the twentieth century, we are better placed than historians in the heyday of Victorian Liberalism to understand the sort of pressures to which Cranmer had been subjected."

Cranmer's story has been a part of English-speaking heritage since the publication in 1563 of Foxe's *Book of Martyrs.* Cranmer's unparalleled contribution in the production of the Prayer Book has been well appreciated. However, anachronistic and immature judgments of Cranmer's character have tended to obscure from us the personal genius of humility without which we are unable to apprehend the quality of his gift to us.

An example of Cranmer's unique gift of blending theological substance with simple and moving clarity is the Collect traditionally used on the Second Sunday in Advent.

> Blessed Lord, which hast caused all holy Scriptures to be written for our learning; grant us that we may in such wise hear them, read, mark, learn, and inwardly digest them; that by patience and comfort of thy holy word, we may embrace, and ever hold fast the blessed hope of everlasting life, which thou hast given us in our savior Jesus Christ.

This prayer has been so universally appreciated across denominational lines (by people mostly unaware of its origin) that the Second Sunday in Advent was chosen by Protestant bodies throughout the world as "Bible Sunday." Like the General Confession below, this is no mere created piece of individual eloquence, but a compilation of phrases and significant terms of Scripture.

Cranmer's prayers are saturated with Scripture and they are compiled with such economy and clarity that in no sense could one say that they had been merely "written." The very best example is the General Confession in the services of Morning and Evening Prayer:

Almighty and most merciful Father; We have erred, and strayed from thy ways like lost sheep. We have followed too much the devices and desires of our own hearts. We have offended against thy holy laws. We have left undone those things which we ought to have done; And we have done those things which we ought not to have done; and there is no health in us. But thou, O Lord, have mercy upon us, miserable offenders. Spare thou those who are penitent; According to thy promises declared unto mankind in Christ Jesus our Lord. And grant, O most merciful Father, for his sake; That we may hereafter live a godly, righteous, and sober life, to the glory of thy holy Name. Amen

Professor Massey Shepherd has pointed out that this confession is based upon St. Paul's analysis of sin in Romans 7:8-25. In order of their occurrence, the sources are from Isaiah, Psalms, I Peter, Proverbs, Jeremiah, II Chronicles, Matthew, Psalms, Luke, Psalms, Nehemiah, Psalms, Romans, I John, Titus, and John.

The General Confession clearly shows Cranmer's genius of humility. His vision was so unhampered and unclouded by personal ambition or worldly concerns that he could absorb the revelation of God's Word written, digest it in his mind, and appropriate it in his heart. Revelation then flowed into the simple economy of one paragraph with the aforementioned phrases from sixteen biblical sources in eight short sentences. Subsequent generations have been given a unique biblical vision through a vehicle hammered out in the blend of thought and passion, trust and faith of Cranmer's life.

The theme of repentance runs through Cranmer's liturgy. His very character was rooted and founded in humility before God. This is why God continues to speak and reveal himself to millions around the world (many who have never heard Cranmer's name) after 450 years of using the traditional English liturgy. Not even through the contributions of Augustine, Luther, Calvin, or Wesley does the revelation of God come so unclouded and uncolored by the personality of the medium.

The personality and character of Cranmer is marked by a Christian virtue that a secular age cannot fathom. Humility before God is a transcendent and eschatological virtue that depends upon the "sure and certain hope" of eternal life. Before God (*coram Deo*) we can never depend on our own worth but on the mercies of Christ.

The figure of the Cardinal in Bridget Boland's play *The Prisoner* is asked by his interrogator why he does not choose to take his own life rather than face the multitude to whom he has been manipulated into confessing falsely to horrendous crimes and who are now judging him. His reply is simply, "He who made me is he who will be my judge." It is ironic that amendments to the play have eliminated the factors of the Cardinal's weakness and the movie was banned in Ireland. This humility before God is seen in a Sadducean (no resurrection) age as weak and obsequious. Yet, for Cranmer and for other believers, the mercy and forgiveness of God is the final and everlasting word for Christians.

Cranmer's sainthood cannot be established on the grounds of sinlessness or denial of weakness, which is an adolescent expectation. He loved life and retained a real measure of the fear of death. The Church, quite early, learned a danger of martyrdom as escape, when some were tempted to give their lives, not so much as witness, but as release from the ambiguities of life and to gain the joys of heaven prematurely.

The Christian paradox, that God uses the weak to confound the strong, can be seen in the life of Cranmer, where strength is above weakness. However, the paradox can be read the other way. There is strength beneath weakness which is obscure to a secular age (cf. II Corinthians 11:30ff.)

There is something everlastingly encouraging about Cranmer's faithful death. All who suffer injustice, betrayal, and defeat of what seems fair and good and according to the purpose of God himself can consider the mind of Cranmer as he died. The burning, dying Cranmer saw nothing with his natural eyes but a bleak Friday with the complete and utter failure and destruction of all he believed in. The unseen Easter reality was Queen Elizabeth's restoration of all his accomplishments and their abiding nurture over subsequent centuries. They were things hoped for but unseen by Cranmer, perceived only by the eye of faith and a heart of hope, faith and trust in the providence of God that gave Cranmer his courage in those last hours.

C. FitzSimons Allison
XII Bishop of South Carolina

Notes to the Reader

The title of this book is *The Collects of Thomas Cranmer,* but the reader will soon discover that the archbishop (and his fellow revisers) were basically editors and translators of the old Sacramentary Collects of the fifth and sixth centuries. Only a few were composed specifically for the first Book of Common Prayer (1549). Readers will also note that the Collects survived fairly intact through the 1928 American Prayer Book. The 1979 Book retains a number of them, though not necessarily on their original day.

We have retained the (by modern standards) somewhat inconsistent punctuation and capitalization of the original Cranmerian versions, but have modernized the spelling for ease of reading. We have chosen only the Sunday Collects and a few for Holy Days. Editions of the Book of Common Prayer cited or considered in this volume are those of 1549, 1552, 1559, and 1662 (England); and 1789, 1892, 1928, and 1979 (U.S.A.).

For historical notes, we have relied heavily on the following resources, with special acknowledgment to the work of the Rev. L. E. H. Stephens-Hodge, and the great treasure given the Church by Dr. Massey Shepherd.

The First and Second Prayer Books of Edward VI (London: Dent, 1910).

The Oxford American Prayer Book Commentary, by Massey Hamilton Shepherd, Jr. (New York: Oxford University Press, 1950).

L. E. H. Stephens-Hodge, *The Collects (London: Hodder and Stoughton, 1961).*

Evan Daniel, *The Prayer-Book; Its History, Language and Contents* (London: Wells, Gardner, Darton, & Co., 1883).

Francis Procter, revised and rewritten by Walter Howard Frere, *A New History of the Book of Common Prayer with a Rationale of Its Offices* (London: MacMillan and Co., Ltd., 1885, 1901).

W. K. Lowther Clarke and Charles Harris, eds., *Liturgy and Worship: A Companion to the Prayer Books of the Anglican Communion* (London: S.P.C.K., 1950).

Diarmaid MacCullough, *Thomas Cranmer: A Life* (New Haven: Yale University Press, 1996).

The editors wish to give special thanks to Mrs. Nita Moorhead for her tireless assistance in the production of this book.

THE COLLECTS
OF
THOMAS CRANMER

The First Sunday in Advent

THE COLLECT

lmighty God, give us grace, that we may cast away the works of darkness, and put upon us the armor of light, now in the time of this mortal life, (in the which thy son Jesus Christ came to visit us in great humility;) that in the last day when he shall come again in his glorious majesty to judge both the quick and the dead, we may rise to the life immortal, through him who liveth and reigneth with thee and the holy ghost now and ever. Amen.

HISTORY

The Christian year has not always begun with the First Sunday in Advent. The earliest "beginning" was Easter Day, a custom still observed in the great Churches of the East. By the fourth century, the West had established Christmas Day as the beginning of the ecclesiastical year. A time of preparation for Epiphany baptisms began on St. Martin's Day (November 11). This came to be known as Advent, leading up to Christ's coming, and was later shortened to four weeks before Christmas (beginning the Sunday closest to St. Andrew's Day), just as we have it today.

The Collect for Advent I (and enjoined to be read each day of Advent in the 1662 revision) was composed by Archbishop Cranmer for the 1549 Prayer Book. Like other Reformation Collects, it is based on the Epistle (Romans 13:8-14) and Gospel (St. Matthew 21:1-13) which follow.

MEDITATION

Tying together the beginning and the ending of our lives: How can we do it? Can we understand our life's course, all its fantastic ebbings and flowings, as one whole, and not as a thousand separated memories and episodes? Or when our life passes before us as it does in the split second before an accident, is it just a succession of scenes, set pieces with no running theme or meaning? Am I the person who was born with my name? And when I lay dying, will I be able to make sense of the question, how did I come to be here?

The Collect for the First Sunday in Advent achieves an astonishing feat. It ties together not only the first coming and the final coming of God — the two advents of Jesus Christ — but it binds together our human present with the future, which is even now rushing towards us.

The prayer asks Almighty God for grace to do the right thing, even the works of love, "in the time of this mortal life." "I need thee ev'ry hour" (*The Hymnal 1940*, number 438), and this hour in particular! Moreover, my present world, so conflicted by the "works of darkness," was once visited. The world was hallowed by the visitation of the Son and therefore is hallowed still. I am accompanied during the present moment in my hope of becoming an angel of light to others.

Yet the future is also coming towards us in all its "glorious majesty." And then, our life today, fraught and ambiguous at every lived level of it, will be swallowed up in victory (I Corinthians 15:54). That victory is represented in the Collect as "the life immortal."

The point of this first prayer devised by Cranmer for the Christian year is that our present life is the incubator for our future and enduring life. And every moment of this life is accompanied by Him who visited the planet in great humility.

Do you see your life as a unity, a kind of oneness, even in the midst of rags and patches, its experienced many-ness? You are even today the person who was born with your name years ago and you are at the same time the person who will live forever in the Kingdom of God. Your life has inexhaustible meaning.

The Second Sunday in Advent

THE COLLECT

lessed Lord, which hast caused all holy Scriptures to be written for our learning; grant us that we may in such wise hear them, read, mark, learn, and inwardly digest them; that by patience and comfort of thy holy word, we may embrace, and ever hold fast the blessed hope of everlasting life, which thou hast given us in our savior Jesus Christ.

HISTORY

A new emphasis on Holy Scripture at the time of the English Reformation is seen in this Collect, which is an original composition of Archbishop Cranmer. His Preface to the 1549 Prayer Book (and retained in the current American Prayer Book under "Historical Documents") is well worth reading. He describes the situation inherited by the Reformers: the venerable practice of reading the whole Bible through in a year of public worship had become "altered, broken, and neglected."

The form of the Collect is unique: the address is made to the Father as "Blessed Lord," and the pleading clause is missing at the end. The present ending (Colossians 1:27) reflects the belief that every part of Scripture bears witness in some way to Jesus Christ.

MEDITATION

This prayer carries forward the theme of unity with which Cranmer started the cycle on the preceding Sunday. In the first week's prayer, our human present was linked with our immortal future through the two advents of Christ. Today the emphasis rests on a reference point, a text, which exists as a compass to orient our whole lives.

To whom do you refer when you are trying to prove a point? Do you refer to your father, to your extremely wise mother, to a mentor, to the Founding Fathers, to Dr. King, to the rector, to the previous rector, to the winner of a Nobel prize? Or is there a source book or touchstone to settle the question: Webster's Dictionary, the Internet, the works of Dickens, *Citizen Kane*, *Time* magazine, the Guinness Book of Records?

For Cranmer, the touchstone or reference point for wisdom is "all holy Scriptures." He prays that we would not only hear the Scriptures as words, but "inwardly digest" them as the Word by which we may be comforted (i.e., strengthened). Cranmer views the Bible as providing both the grounds for our patience and the fuel for our strengthening. Such patience and strengthening are able to take us by the instrumentality of hope right up to the threshold of natural life. After we cross that threshold, we shall receive the "everlasting life" promised in the last phrase.

The reference point of Scripture gives the gift of unity to our otherwise scattered experience of life, life as a sequence of episodes roughly edited by the passage of time. The Word, learned and felt, then tried by experience, accompanies us, just as last Sunday's Collect related the accompaniment of One who visited us in great humility.

"Thy Word is a lamp unto my feet" (Psalm 119:105).

In *The Apostle*, a 1998 film by Robert Duvall, the hero strings up a neon-lit arrow, almost like a rocketship, on the belfry of a little country church where he has started to preach. The sign says, in letters going up vertically, "One Way Road to Heaven Church." Garish as it is, the sign is an arresting beacon. It lights the landscape of the movie, as do the Scriptures, Old and New Testament, for us.

Cranmer invites us to love the Bible and learn it, not for its own sake, but for the sake of the cause for which it was written: our patience and our comfort.

The Third Sunday in Advent

THE COLLECT

ord, we beseech thee, give ear to our prayers, and by thy gracious visitation lighten the darkness of our heart, by our Lord Jesus Christ.

HISTORY

This brief prayer is medieval in origin and was translated by the archbishop for use in the 1549 Prayer Book. It survived there just over a century, being replaced in 1662 by a Collect reflecting both the coming Advent Ember Days and the appointed Epistle and Gospel for Advent III.

MEDITATION

Do you see your heart as dark? Has your heart, the core of your emotions, ever become darkened or closed to new light through some unforgettable hurt? Do you remember with any conviction the old Burt Bacharach tune, "I'll Never Fall in Love Again," with its ironically "light" melody? Do you know what it is to have been hurt in such a way that the scar tissue is now fixed and hard, obstructing and closing in your love upon itself? Like Miss Havisham in *Great Expectations,* whose jilting in her twenties became an inoperable tumor through to her sixties!

The succinct Collect for the Third Sunday in Advent assumes that our human heart has become dark. The Collect presupposes that by the time we reach the point where we should wish to pray this prayer, we would have found, by the sheer passage of years and chronicle of love's disappointments, that our open and bright self had seized up. A personality once sunny and receptive could discover itself in the arid place of wishing to shut out the joy and light of life, let alone the grace of God, entirely.

The prayer sees the answer to our darkness as the light shining in the face of Christ (II Corinthians 4:6). "By thy gracious visitation, lighten the darkness." Are you able to see the darkness of life's conflictedness as dispelled by the ancient yet still present accompaniment of God-with-us? This is the love which pierces the darkness, even when you and I have covered over our windows, the eyes of our heart, with hammered shutters, wooden boards, duct tape, and clear-for-all-to-read "no trespassing" signs.

Our Christian hope opposes the finality of Miss Havisham's position.

The Fourth Sunday in Advent

THE COLLECT

ord raise up (we pray thee) thy power, and come among us, and with great might succor us; that whereas, through our sins and wickedness, we be sore let and hindered, thy bountiful grace and mercy, through the satisfaction of thy son our Lord, may speedily deliver us; to whom with thee and the holy ghost be honor and glory, world without end.

HISTORY

This Collect is from the Gelasian Sacramentary, an early Roman Missal or prayer book. It was, in turn, absorbed into the Sarum (i.e., Salisbury) liturgy, from which Archbishop Cranmer translated and adapted it for use in the 1549 Prayer Book. It was expanded in the 1662 Book to include the phrase "running the race that is set before us," thus linking up with Hebrews 12:1. "Succor" means to run to the assistance of someone. "Let" in this case is a word which means today the exact opposite of its sixteenth-century meaning. To be "sore let" is to be thwarted. For other examples see Isaiah 43:13 and Romans 1:13 (King James Version).

MEDITATION

Cranmer's panoramic vision and sense of the big picture of our life as "hid with Christ" (Colossians 3:3) comes through loud and clear in this prayer. Many of the collects carry this dense feeling for human life from its birth to its eternal destiny after death.

The prayer represents us as being hindered through our sins and wickedness. We are thwarted in all our attempts at self-deliverance. That is a grievous admission. We are unable to help ourselves: trapped, stripped, caught by outward circumstances and inward tendencies. This is as it were a paraphrase of Step One of the Twelve Steps. Our life is fundamentally out of control! No one can appreciate the power of this prayer without first making the admission that all human hopes of self-redemption are a delusion. Is that too much to admit?

But as we are "sore hindered," even so is the mercy of God bountiful and speedy. Moreover, the mercy of God is not a facile fiat. It is grounded in something: "the satisfaction of thy Son our Lord." You could have all the faith in the world in thin ice, but you would still fall through. You could have extremely fragile faith in thick ice, and you would not fall through. The thick ice which will not give way is the historic sacrifice of Christ on the Cross, satisfying the Judge of Life. With sins forgiven, the human spirit is no longer obstructed and caved in on its own insatiable hungers. There is breathing room, known in St. Paul's Letter to the Galatians as liberty (chapter 5, verse 1).

Christmas Day

THE FIRST COLLECT

God, which makest us glad with the yearly remembrance of the birth of thy only son Jesus Christ; grant that as we joyfully receive him for our redeemer, so we may with sure confidence behold him, when he shall come to be our judge, who liveth and reigneth, &c.

THE SECOND COLLECT
(also to be used on the Sunday after Christmas Day)

Almighty God, which hast given us thy only begotten son to take our nature upon him, and this day to be born of a pure Virgin; Grant that we being regenerate, and made thy children by adoption and grace, may daily be renewed by thy holy spirit, through the same our Lord Jesus Christ who liveth and reigneth with thee and the holy ghost now and ever. Amen.

HISTORY

Christmas (cristmasse, Christ's Mass) is a term first used in the twelfth century. The feast itself was introduced in Rome in the fourth century in order to establish a Christian festival to replace the old pagan festival of the birth of the sun god (winter solstice).

Two Collects for the Feast are provided in the 1549 Prayer Book. The First Collect is a translation from the Gregorian Sacramentary (sixth century), one of the early forms of the Roman liturgy. It passed into use at the Cathedral in Salisbury as the Collect for the Vigil of Christmas. It was from this "Sarum Rite" that Cranmer developed his English adaptation.

The Second Collect, an original composition of Cranmer, is profoundly biblical, as are all the Reformation Collects. It reminds us of our status as God's "children by adoption and grace," while Christ alone is His "only begotten Son." It is, of all the Prayer Book Collects, the most profoundly theological. Here in one superb prayer are contained both the doctrine of the Holy Trinity and the Incarnation of Christ in time and in our souls.

MEDITATION

The Good News of the Gospel affirms that God is both for us and with us. His being for us means that He does something on our behalf that we cannot do for ourselves. This *for-us-ness* refers to the Atonement, by which Christ died for us in our place on the Cross, thereby sparing us from judgment and guilt.

God's *with-us-ness* means that He has "taken our nature upon him," to accompany us as friend and shepherd during the pilgrimage of living. This *with-us-ness* refers to the Incarnation, by which God is born into the world and shares the condition of human beings with the single exception of sin. ". . . And he feeleth for our sadness, and he shareth in our gladness" (Cecil Frances Alexander, 1848).

The two Collects for Christmas are so arranged as to give priority in order of time to the *for*-ness of Christ. The prayer for the First Communion of Christmas stresses the Atonement. But Christ's *with-ness* is also celebrated, in the prayer for the Second Communion of the Day, which stresses the Incarnation.

Is it not this way in life? We are aided at an acute point of need by someone. Then, just afterwards, when the immediate crisis is past, we start asking, "Who was that who helped us?" Remember the Lone Ranger. He rode into town with Tonto and cleaned up the place. At the end of every episode, someone always asked, "Who was that masked man?"

It is the same with Christ. He comes to our aid, love unlocks our prison, grace embraces our weakness, and we are undone, in the most potentially fruitful sense. Very soon after the break-in of grace, we wish to know more. Then, later, we cannot ask enough questions!

This is how the Christian Doctrine of God began. It is also how the doctrine of the Holy Trinity took shape. Who was it that came to my aid, in my concrete life? Anyone who could help me that much must be extremely unusual. Divine, in fact. Certainly worthy of my bended knee.

Cranmer's ordering of the Collects for Christmas Day is important, even moving. Redemption precedes speculation, the freeing act of God precedes reflection about Him. In historical theology, both concretely personal and abstractly universal, Atonement precedes Incarnation. I have been helped, therefore I believe. God is for me, therefore He is with me.

11

The Circumcision of Christ

THE COLLECT

lmighty God, which madest thy blessed son to be circumcised, and obedient to the law for man; Grant us the true circumcision of thy spirit, that our hearts, and all our members, being mortified from all worldly and carnal lusts, may in all things obey thy blessed will; through the same thy son Jesus Christ our Lord.

HISTORY

This Collect, based on Romans 2:29, Colossians 3:5, and Titus 2:12, was taken from the Gregorian Sacramentary. As early as the sixth century, it was considered a fast day, as opposed to the pagan carnival of New Year's Day. The "station Mass" in Rome on this day was at the basilica in the Jewish quarter of the city, an obvious source for the emphasis on the Circumcision. It is ironic that in today's era of supposed frankness, the title has been changed to "The Holy Name."

MEDITATION

A constant struggle in the Christian life is the interplay between inward and outward. Jesus spoke of whited sepulchres, "which indeed appear beautiful outward, but are within full of dead men's bones, and of all uncleanness" (St. Matthew 23:27). It is all too sure that we can go through the motions and not mean a word of it!

Jesus was circumcized eight days after his birth, as prescribed by the Law (Genesis 17:12; 21:4). St. Paul spoke later of the "true circumcision" (Romans 4:28, 29), which is inward and of the heart. The parents of Jesus honored the commandment because it was a commandment. We see circumcision as an inward purification, according ideally with the outward actions of life.

When you meditate on a written prayer such as this one, ask yourself first, *what is being asked for here?* When you take away the address ("Almighty God, which . . .") and the formal pleading ("through the same thy son . . ."), what exactly is being prayed for? In this prayer, on the occasion of the Feast of Christ's Circumcision, the petitioner — and we are the petitioner — is asking God for "the true circumcision of thy spirit." The idea is that the Holy Spirit alone can cleanse us and prompt us to accede from the heart to the design of God for our life. A transformed will results in changed actions. The Holy Spirit "circumcises" us from within. The consequence is an inward desire to obey God. Such a will bears the fruit of good works.

Aristotle saw it differently: outward actions change the inward essence of a human being. You become what you do. The tradition represented by the Collect for the Circumcision sees it the other way around. By the use of this Collect, Cranmer plants the Prayer Book on ethical ground that is biblical, and is neither Aristotelian (as in, "we become what we do") nor Platonic (right action follows from right thinking). Cranmer pulls us sharply away from "Greek" or "classical" ideas. What we do results, rather, from who we are, or better, from what the prior grace of God has helped us to become.

13

The Epiphany

THE COLLECT

O God, which by the leading of a star didst manifest thy only begotten son to the Gentiles; Mercifully grant, that we, which know thee now by faith, may after this life have the fruition of thy glorious Godhead; through Christ our Lord.

HISTORY

The Twelfth Day of Christmas concludes the Christmas festivities. Here the Collect, drawn from the Gregorian Sacramentary, has been weakened in Cranmer's translation. The original ending prays that "we who know thee now by faith, may be brought to the contemplation of thy Majesty by sight," thus drawing the contrast between faith and sight (II Corinthians 5:7).

The Greek term *Epiphany* is translated as "appearing" in the New Testament (I Timothy 6:14, II Timothy 4:1, Titus 2:13). The Rev. L. E. H. Stephens-Hodge, in his excellent commentary on the Collects, points out that the themes of the Epiphany Collects may be summarized as follows:

1. *Power* to know and to do God's will   (Epiphany I)
2. *Peace,* spiritual and temporal   (Epiphany II)
3. *Protection* against dangers from without   (Epiphany III)
4. *Protection* against dangers from within   (Epiphany IV)
5. *Protection* for the Church of God   (Epiphany V)
6. *Purity* in conformity with the revealed character of Christ.   (Epiphany VI)

MEDITATION

Do you remember ever seeing or reading Thornton Wilder's play *The Skin of Our Teeth*? Although not so well known as *Our Town*, it is a sort of cosmic drama about how the human race makes it through the course of history, catastrophe, war, and crisis, by "the skin of our teeth."

That is an apt expression to describe the inclusion of the Gentiles in the Kingdom of God. To use the old language, we have been grafted onto the vine of Israel; or, to use the new, by the skin of our teeth. "For I would not, brethren, that ye should be ignorant of this mystery, lest ye should be wise in your own conceits; for blindness in part is happened to Israel, until the fullness of the Gentiles be come in" (Romans 11:25). Our inclusion has nothing to do with us!

The Collect expresses this Pauline mystery of divine undeserved favor, the Epiphany or appearance of the Messiah to the Gentiles, with a bold stroke. The prayer describes the moment of the Magis' discovery of Christ and then turns it right around to us. We are Gentiles who know Christ not by sight, as the Magi did, but by faith.

Moreover, we are not genetically related, most of us, to Israel, from whom the Messiah has sprung. So it is in every sense "by faith," and not by means of something palpable, whether sight or sure inheritance, that we are in relation to God. We are in there "by the skin of our teeth," or rather, by His free decision to make us His. We had nothing to do with it.

The Epiphany: three star-led kings on camels: the skin of our teeth. Please, O God, make it so abidingly.

The First Sunday after the Epiphany

THE COLLECT

ord we beseech thee mercifully to receive the prayers of thy people which call upon thee; and grant that they may both perceive and know what things they ought to do, and also have grace and power faithfully to fulfill the same.

HISTORY

Based on James 4:17, St. John 13:17 and St. Luke 12:47, this Collect was appointed in the Gregorian Sacramentary and was included in the Book of Common Prayer through its use at Salisbury Cathedral. In the Gregorian prayer underlying the Collect, the word translated "prayer" is *vota,* votive offerings, thus linking the Wise Men and their gifts to the Epistle originally appointed for this day: Romans 12:1-5.

MEDITATION

What ought I to do? How can I perceive or discern what the right thing to do is, especially when there is more than one real possibility?

Moreover, if I am given to know what to do in the midst of quandary, how can I do it? Will I have gas in the engine to follow through on what I know to be right? Or, knowing full well the right direction, will I sputter and stall at the starting line?

This prayer is a model of verticality. Vertical prayer is prayer that is not horizontal. Vertical prayer does not speak to the people around you, as in, "O Lord, our friend here has a problem and will you make sure he does the right thing" (which you, the petitioner, have already decided — and are suggesting!). Rather, the Collect makes no presumptions or assumptions. It takes us straight to God. The prayer is entirely without judgment. It puts the matter of "the right thing to do" squarely between the speaker and the Listener. This shows that in prayer, prior judgments are out!

All the Collect asks of God is that He hear or "receive" the asking, and that He help the one who prays to perceive what he or she ought to do. And whatever that turns out to be, to aid the person in doing it. A more succinct, less pompous prayer could scarcely exist. Pray it today, specifically in that area of confusion where you really do not know what to do. If the prayer is spoken as open-endedly as it is written, you will get your answer.

The Second Sunday after the Epiphany

THE COLLECT

lmighty and everlasting God, which dost govern all things in heaven and earth: mercifully hear the supplications of thy people, and grant us thy peace all the days of our life.

HISTORY

The original Latin form of this petition was for outward peace, "peace in our time," as reflected in the suffrage of Morning and Evening Prayer, "Give peace in our time, O Lord." Archbishop Cranmer's version suggests instead that peace which the world cannot give (St. John 14:27). We remember the stormy times in which this prayer was translated and adapted for English use.

MEDITATION

Would you be able to affirm with anything like solid confidence that God "governs all things in heaven and earth"?

Granted, we might affirm it in general terms. We might wish to affirm it in concrete terms. But how many of us would also keep our fingers crossed behind our back?

Does He govern all things in heaven and earth? Or, rather, are there one or two undiscussables, those unprayable matters which bitter defeat and chronic experience have taught us to exempt from the list of things God governs?

There is, for example, the hope of change in that particular difficult person. Ungoverned! There is the thought of improvement in that particular rut I find myself in. Ungoverned! There is the state of the world, the state of the Church, the state of my house, the state of my head, the state of my health. Ungoverned!

What do you exempt, in practice, from the "all things in heaven and earth" which the Collect places under the direction and oversight of Almighty God? If this prayer has any integrity at all, the answer has to be, nothing. That would seem to fly in the face of our personal experience, which continually exempts chronic unprayables from God's oversight.

Consider *un*-exempting the impossible thing that has got you defeated. Consider taking it out from your strongbox of undiscussables and setting it before the Lord one more time. And pray the old words of this Collect. The gift given back should be "peace, all the days of our life."

The Third Sunday after the Epiphany

THE COLLECT

Almighty and everlasting God, mercifully look upon our infirmities, and in all our dangers and necessities, stretch forth thy right hand to help and defend us; through Christ our Lord.

HISTORY

Archbishop Cranmer took this Collect from the Sarum Missal, adding the phrase "in all our dangers and necessities." It originally was matched to the Gospel for the Day (later moved to the Fourth Sunday of the Epiphany), St. Matthew 8:1-13, in which we are told that Jesus *"put forth his hand* and touched him, saying, 'I will, be thou clean.'"

MEDITATION

The prayer, which is terse, asks God to look and help. The desired looking is not detached and it is not analytical. God is asked to look at our weaknesses.

This is important. Would we not rather have Him take a good look at our "strengths"? Would we not rather *shine?*

No, the Collect is composed from the place of need. Morris Maddocks, bishop in the Church of England, has never tired of saying, "God meets us at our point of need." This is the idea here. We are infirm, shaky. Our weaknesses are the cracks and loosened foundations which always render us idols with feet of clay.

In my infirmity, I need helping, to move positively forward through it. I need defending, to hold back the forces (of the world, the flesh, and the devil) that see my weaknesses like gaps in a wall and pour right through them, taking terrible advantage of me. The prayer is therefore both offensive and defensive.

This, too, is the character of Christian faith. It is like Christian's sword in *A Pilgrim's Progress,* which he holds before him. It withstands "the evil day," in the sense of Ephesians 6, with the whole armor of God (verses 11-17). The Christian faith is simultaneously on the offensive and on the defensive.

The Fourth Sunday after the Epiphany

THE COLLECT

God, which knowest us to be set in the midst of so many and great dangers, that for man's frailness we cannot always stand uprightly; Grant to us the health of body and soul that all those things which we suffer for sin, by thy help we may well pass and overcome; through Christ our Lord.

HISTORY

This Collect is based on the Collect for Ember Saturday in Lent in the Gregorian Sacramentary. The "many and great dangers" are, in historical context, a reference to the troubled times of Pope Gregory. Through its alteration by the archbishop in the sixteenth century, the Collect has been made more widely general in its application. The "many and great dangers" also reflect the Gospel appointed for the day (St. Matthew 8:23-27), the storm at sea, a visible point in which the disciples could not "always stand uprightly."

MEDITATION

We are in this prayer both victims of forces outside our control *and* responsible agents and overcomers. How is that possible?

We are victims because we are "set in the midst of so many and great dangers." Moreover, we are depicted as frail, weakened by our nature to the extent that we cannot stand upright. Can anyone realistically deny this? Outward circumstances constitute the curve balls and tight corners of human experience. Inward character traits and inherited flaws, as well as the driest deserts of love rendered waterless by past experience: these inward or character limitations compound and double the trouble which comes from outside. Human beings are caught between outward oppression and inward erosion.

But the prayer asks for health. The petition is singular and for one thing: health of body and soul. The result, according to the Collect, will be successful navigation ("that we may well pass") and even victory. Facing the facts — our "beset"-ness — then asking for help — "grant us . . ." — produce the first fruits of overcoming. The root is aid requested; the fruit, success in reaching port.

Now tell me: Was there ever a better balance between the evidence of victimhood and the hope for change and transformation? Christianity carries the conviction that grace results in responsibility. If we see the true state of things and bring it before God plainly and without rationalization, God answers our prayers. Far from ballooning up with a surfeit of self-righteous victimhood as lifelong policy, we begin to get responsible. We begin to overcome the "great dangers" set before us. Amen.

The Fifth Sunday after the Epiphany

THE COLLECT

L ord, we beseech thee to keep thy Church and household continually in thy true religion; that they which do lean only upon hope of thy heavenly grace may evermore be defended by thy mighty power; through Christ our Lord.

HISTORY

Cranmer appointed this Collect to serve on the succeeding Sunday ("if there be so many"). In 1662 a new Collect was added (by Bishop Cosin?) for the Sixth Sunday.

These two Collects have been called "the wandering collects," to be used either to fill up a long Epiphany season or, if necessary, to be used at the end of Trinity season, their placement being dependent upon the date of Easter in any given year.

The Collect for the Fifth Sunday after the Epiphany is again taken from the Gregorian Sacramentary. The opening phrase is the same (in Latin) as in the Collect for Trinity XXII. In both, Cranmer has placed the word "Church" alongside the word "household" to make the meaning clear. Dr. Shepherd points out that the phrase "continually in thy true religion" represents the Latin *continua pietate,* reflecting God's sentiment towards us, not ours towards Him.

MEDITATION

In this Collect Cranmer sets to rest the question of Christian identity and the correlative question, what is the Church? He defines the Church as "they which do lean only upon hope of thy heavenly grace."

A powerful "either-or" is at work here. The Church is the household of those who have but one single support: the grace of God. "Only" is the key word for us. The only ground on which to place our weight, the only foundation strong enough to take the full burden of all we hope to become as well as all we hope to have forgiven, is God's grace.

A heavy, daunting, awesome thought: it puts all our eggs in one basket! Would you not rather spread your hopes around, at least a little, if only for the sake of insurance? Put at least some hope on your children, or on your friends, or on a Bach fugue or magnificent sunset, for that matter? What is this alarming *only?* The *only* is there because only God's gift from outside ourselves, from outside the human condition, takes the burden entirely off what we bring to the equation.

This is because what human beings bring is always flawed. Nothing we do or can do or be is perfect. Therefore nothing a person can do will withstand the perfect examination of God, who is by definition perfect. St. Peter said, "Depart from me, O Lord, for I am a sinful man" (St. Luke 5:8).

This particular Collect cuts it close. Because it is close. Only the whole perfection of God, deployed and arranged on our side, is sufficient to ground our hopes of an ultimately clean slate, and also unending life. Will you stand on the secure foundation of this *only?*

The Sunday called Septuagesima

THE COLLECT

O Lord, we beseech thee favorably to hear the prayers of thy people; that we which are justly punished for our offenses, may be mercifully delivered by thy goodness, for the glory of thy name, through Jesus Christ our Savior, who liveth and reigneth, &c.

HISTORY

The three Pre-Lenten Sundays passed into Prayer Book use from the medieval rite. They reflect the perilous condition of Italy at the time of Pope Gregory, which was threatened by barbarian invasions, and the plagues, famine, and earthquakes of that era.

The names of these Sundays are Septuagesima (approximately seventy days before Easter), Sexagesima (approximately sixty) days before Easter, and Quinquagesima (exactly fifty days before Easter). This countdown for the forty days of Lent prepares us for "the time of fast and prayer, that with hearts made penitent, we may keep a faithful Lent" (Katherine Hankey, 1888).

MEDITATION

The stress is always and consistently throughout the Prayer Book Collects on the redemption side of religion. This stress, persistent and unfailing, on what God does for us sinners, can prove intolerable to modern ears. In fact, the redemption emphasis has been softened in modern revisions, often in favor of an emphasis on "creation." It might be possible to say that the Collects in their original form are downright morbid in their monocular focus on judgment and deliverance.

Unless . . . it were true. Unless it were true that human beings really do exist under judgment and the fear of judgment. Unless it were true that the great question of life is the question of forgiveness and acquittal.

I believe we can affirm Cranmer's dogged emphasis from our own experience. This writer does. There is no feeling more draining (or more drenching) than the feeling that one has fallen short and failed to live up to what is expected of us. We are convinced that a cardinal task of living is the *recovery* of "Type-A" personalities from the overwhelming power of demand, which the world today calls stress. The answer to the Type-A dilemma is not to pull up stakes and move over to the country of the Type-Bs. They have their own problems, the other side of the coin to the ferocious Type-As.

But to be able to move out from judgment and unremitting demand as the motivating engine of life: what a glorious hope.

This prayer, for Septuagesima, is for us. We certainly live under the sign of shortfall, inadequacy, and what the Collect represents as the just punishment for our offenses. We pray here for merciful deliverance by God. We pray for acquittal and remission, granted by virtue of Another's action. Will you observe how universal and therefore contemporary this prayer really is?

The Sunday called Sexagesima

THE COLLECT

ord God, which seest that we put not our trust in any thing that we do; mercifully grant that by thy power we may be defended against all adversity; through Jesus Christ our Lord.

HISTORY

This Collect is taken from the Gregorian Sacramentary, but the archbishop deleted the phrase "by the protection of the Doctor of the Gentiles" after the word "defended." This was a reference to the Mass celebrated on Sexagesima by the Pope at St. Paul's Basilica on the Ostian Way, where the Apostle to the Gentiles was buried. This theme is reflected in the Epistle for the Day (II Corinthians 11:19-31).

MEDITATION

Non nobis, domine: "Not unto us, O Lord, not unto us, but unto thy name give the glory, for thy mercy, and for thy truth's sake" (Psalm 115:1). This was one of the Reformers' favorite texts.

Biblical religion could almost be summed up by that one verse. We cannot take the credit for any good thing in the world. Every good thing is from above (James 1:17). It all comes under the signature of gift.

Is that a little extreme? Is it anti-humane, or antihuman, referring all worthy things to a source outside ourselves? The prayer sounds severe.

But it is what Scripture says. It is also what Cranmer wishes us to hear: "Lord God, which seest that we put not our trust in any thing that we do." God sees to it that we put not our trust in such things, because every created thing lets us down when we serve it rather than the One who made it. God sees to it, by means of "2×4 religion" (because it takes the "2×4" of experience to pound in the message), that our fingers are pulled one by one away from their grasp on penultimate goods.

God also sees us when we put our trust in Him. He observes us, implies the prayer, as we refocus our trust upon that which is trustworthy: the grace of God. Then the prayer for "defense against adversity" becomes the most natural prayer in the world.

This Collect is a frontal assault on every "other god," on "the dearest idol I have known" (William Cowper, 1772). Are your idols crumbling to dust before your eyes? That is the intention.

The Sunday called Quinquagesima

THE COLLECT

Lord which dost teach us that all our doings without charity are nothing worth; send thy holy ghost, and pour into our hearts that most excellent gift of charity, the very bond of peace and all virtues, without the which whosoever liveth is counted dead before thee: Grant this for thy only son, Jesus Christ's sake.

HISTORY

This Collect is an original composition of Thomas Cranmer, replacing the medieval prayer which asked that "we, being absolved from the chain of our sins, may be defended from all adversity." That reference was to the special confession of Shrove Tuesday in which the faithful were "shriven" or absolved of their sins.

Our Reformers believed that such outward observances fall short of what we might call "religion of the heart." Thus Cranmer created a new Collect based on the Epistle which would follow, St. Paul's hymn to love in I Corinthians 13.

MEDITATION

The Collect returns us to the theme of either-or. Either we are alive or we are dead (St. Luke 15:24, 32). Either we are found or we are lost (15:6, 9). Either we see or we are blind (St. John 9:25). And here, in the context of this prayer, we are without charity "counted dead before thee." Moreover "all our doings without charity" are worth absolutely nothing ("nothing worth")!

This immense either-or at the heart of Christianity is alarming in the extreme. It concedes nothing to slow improvement, to what is called meliorism, or to the idea that life is in essence a process, a journey, even a pilgrimage. Not one of the familiar metaphors of gradualism counts here.

This implies a pessimistic, better a tragic estimation of the human condition. Which is to say, it asserts that on its own terms or in the initial situation of its sorry givenness, the problem of being human is a closed system. Our human nature being what it is, the world's work is of zero moral worth.

On the other hand, with the gift of divine love we are able to achieve the works of love which carry true value and worth. With the gift of charity come peace and all the other virtues. Love enlivens every action. Love builds a unity of purposeful self-giving out of a patchwork of unintegrated "works and days" (Hesiod, eighth century B.C.). The Collect wishes to say that with love we are counted alive before God.

You and I have seen this to be true. When an action towards us mirrors genuine caring, it hits its mark: it reaches us. When a word pronounced in our direction is intended for our good, we listen.

The Collect is extreme, and it is also right.

The first day of Lent,
commonly called Ash Wednesday

THE COLLECT

Almighty and everlasting God, which hatest nothing that thou hast made, and dost forgive the sins of all them that be penitent; Create and make in us new and contrite hearts, that we worthily lamenting our sins, and acknowledging our wretchedness, may obtain of thee, the God of all mercy, perfect remission and forgiveness; through Jesus Christ.

HISTORY

This is a new Collect composed by Cranmer to replace one which emphasized fasting rather than repentance. The discontinuance at the Reformation of the medieval custom of sprinkling of ashes on the forehead as a sign of humiliation (so clearly out of place given the Gospel appointed for the day — St. Matthew 6:16-21) necessitated a new Collect.

MEDITATION

The key to hearing this Collect in a fresh and vital mode is its opening description of God, "which hatest nothing that thou hast made." We have seen in Cranmer's scheme, which has negated the presumption of human nature to achieve the good, an express negation of natural effort, of natural temperament, and even of natural gifts. But it is not nihilism that is at work here. Despite the closed-system of the natural world, God nevertheless hates nothing He has made. God's negation of our presumption is preface to his affirmation of the rightly diagnosed human person. He forgives the sins of "all them that be penitent": that is, He restores to the sunlight and "yes" of His presence everyone who "gets" the diagnosis. Penitence means seeing things as they are and flinging back that discouraging truth to God to take care of and dispose.

Can you take the very worst situation of your life, the lowest point to which you have ever seen yourself sink, and still believe that God is reaching towards you? In extremes God is there. It is easy to say this in the abstract. But in the concrete hell of a personal box canyon, it is a genuine tractor beam of fathomless light.

The poet Fulke Greville (1554-1628) said it perfectly and purely, and for us today.

> Down in the depth of mine iniquity,
> That ugly centre of infernal spirits;
> Where each sin feels her own deformity,
> In these peculiar torments she inherits,
>   Depriv'd of human graces, and divine,
>   Even there appears this loving God of mine.

The First Sunday in Lent

THE COLLECT

O Lord, which for our sake didst fast forty days and forty nights; Give us grace to use such abstinence, that, our flesh being subdued to the spirit, we may ever obey thy Godly motions in righteousness, and true holiness, to thy honor and glory, which liveth and reigneth, &c.

HISTORY

Like the Collects of Advent III and St. Stephen's Day, this prayer is addressed directly to Our Lord Jesus Christ. The reason is clear: Hebrews 4:15.

This is an original composition for the 1549 Prayer Book. Our Reformers eliminated the medieval Collect which stressed fasting and good works as a means to earn merit, a notion completely out of line with the New Testament.

MEDITATION

It is clear from this Collect that we cannot obey God in the direction of "righteousness and true holiness" until we are "subdued." What is in mind is the self-control of a person as St. Paul commends it in II Timothy 1:7: "For God hath not given us a spirit of fear; but of power, and of love, and of self-control" ("of a sound mind" in the Authorized Version).

There is a proper sense of having your emotions under rein which precedes any effective service outwards. You have to be free from ungoverned outbreaks of personal need and personal pain if your attempted works of love are not to be marred by self-interest and self-service, even self-sabotage.

The older or medieval model in commending self-control was the model of warfare, the war between the "flesh" and the "spirit." It was as if we were divided between a good "spirit" and a rotten "flesh," the two being ever in conflict like the Three Faces of Eve!

What Cranmer intends here, in place of the old model of warfare between "flesh" and "spirit," is the discipline exercised upon the whole person by the Spirit of God. Through the Spirit it becomes natural rather than against nature to restrain the evil impulse for the sake of love. The "godly motion" of the Collect is the spirit of a man or woman that has been aligned into ways of goodness by the virtue of God's grace preceding.

We are not understood here as being divided in some schizoid or dualistic manner, but rather as persons to be realigned or integrated by the rod of God exercised *from* love and hence *for* love.

Remember the old saw, "The spirit is willing, but the flesh is weak"? Cast out that thought, like the sad rag it is! Exchange it for the glad rag: "Love subdues the spirit, and the 'motions' follow and follow and follow."

The Second Sunday in Lent

THE COLLECT

lmighty God, which dost see that we have no power of our-selves to help ourselves; keep thou us both outwardly in our bodies, and inwardly in our souls; that we may be defended from all adversities which may happen to the body, and from all evil thoughts which may assault and hurt the soul; through Jesus Christ, &c.

HISTORY

This and the remaining Lenten Collects are not originals of Arch-bishop Cranmer, but rather enter the Prayer Book from the Grego-rian Sacramentary by way of the Sarum Rite. We continue to see re-flected not only the troubled times of sixth-century Italy, when they were composed, but also the times of the Reformation in which they were translated.

MEDITATION

The progression of the thought here is, like so many of the Collects, both devastating to the human being on his own terms, and at the same time hopeful.

First, we admit to God the plain fact that "we have no power of ourselves to help ourselves." Is this plain? Is it obvious? Or is it a fact subject to dispute? Step One of the Twelve Steps concurs. World history concurs — at least if you reckon that wars and holocausts in the twentieth century took more lives than every single conflict in the nineteen centuries preceding. Your personal history probably concurs, at least if you have ever been mired in a hole so deep that left to the devices and desires of your own heart you could only sink further into it. The Collect hinges on our earnest if reluctant agreement with the first point.

Second, we are asking God, who exists outside us, to keep us. Why speak to Him if He exists within us? Why differentiate an "I" from a "Thou" if He is not external to us, *extra nos*? We petition God to keep us safe externally (Psalm 91) and also safe within ourselves (Psalm 32). Hold us, grasp us, claim us, do not let us slip through Your fingers like an eely tadpole or like grains of sand.

Third, such keeping, or safekeeping, should result in the best defense. Again, the request is dual: defend us from all outward assault and defend us from all inward temptation. More emphasis — more words in the phrase — is placed on the "evil thoughts" than on the bodily adversities. This is typical of the Prayer Book's worldview. The inner life is more important than the outward experience because it is more lasting. You can be a shell of yourself and still be noble and beloved. You can be a spectacular physique, a true specimen, and be contemptible and alone.

The Collect devastates the human control factor and sets limitless hope upon the sure hold of God.

The Third Sunday in Lent

THE COLLECT

e beseech thee, almighty God, look upon the hearty desires of thy humble servants, and stretch forth the right hand of thy majesty, to be our defence against all our enemies; through Jesus Christ our Lord.

HISTORY

This Collect is taken from the Sacramentary of Gregory and consists of prayer that God will "look upon our heart's desires" and "defend us" against our enemies, both physical and particularly spiritual. It is a reference to the Gospel appointed for the day, St. Luke 11:14-20.

MEDITATION

The governing phrase here is "the hearty desires of thy humble servants," in particular the word "hearty."

This writer recalls with affection the "Hammer Films" made in England during the late 1950s and early 1960s. Evil pagan priests, whether they were from Egypt or Bombay or Haiti, gave little speeches in the context of these melodramatic movies that sounded straight out of the 1662 Prayer Book. They were! The English scriptwriters for Hammer Studios knew only such exalted words to put in the mouths of religious speakers, even if the speakers were sinister cult-priests. Such villains were usually pitted against righteous and very Christian characters played by Peter Cushing or André Morell.

But there was always a difference in the words the villains were given to say and the words found in the Prayer Book itself. Here the difference would consist in the word "hearty." We are not praying to a god in order to achieve our particular desires or conceits. We are not asking a dreamed divinity to do our own bidding. We are praying from the vantage of a "broken and contrite heart" (Psalm 51:17). This is the meaning that stands behind Cranmer's "hearty." Our heart is looking for consolation and trust, the restoration of hope. We petition the Lord from the desire that He will restore our hearts to aspire to what is good, not perform for us what is specific to our grandiose wishes for self-enhancement.

Ask God for you to be given the heart referred to in the Psalter. Then the murmur of your heart will be linked with God's eternal purpose. And what could be more grand?

The Fourth Sunday in Lent

THE COLLECT

rant, we beseech thee, almighty God, that we, which for our evil deeds are worthily punished, by the comfort of thy grace may mercifully be relieved; through our Lord and Savior Jesus Christ.

HISTORY

As with other Lenten collects, this is an English translation of a Collect from the Gregorian Sacramentary. The use of the word "relieved" (i.e., "refreshed," Latin *respiremus*), together with the Gospel (St. John 6:1-14), has given this day the popular title of Refreshment Sunday. Another title for this mid-Lent Sunday is "Mothering Sunday," a reference to the Epistle ("But Jerusalem which is above is free, which is the mother of us all," Galatians 4:26) and to the custom of visiting the mother church of the diocese on this day.

MEDITATION

This is surely one of the least "modern" collects to be found among those included by Cranmer in the 1549 Book. It is one of the least modern prayers, in fact, that we could possibly pray, anywhere or anytime. It posits an untenable situation: "that we . . . do worthily deserve to be punished." It posits the wrath of God.

The situation is both unbearable and at the same time strangely liberating. It is unbearable because: "If thou, Lord, wilt be extreme to mark what is done amiss, O Lord, who may abide it?" (Psalm 130:3) This is a scalpel to the "normal" human posture of self-deception, self-promotion, and self-involvement.

Once in a group of fairly demoralized parish clergy, a visiting bishop from overseas kept referring in his talk to "the Gospel." It was clear that this religious man's words were proving to be uncomfortable in the midst of some pretty weary, depressed, and even cynical rectors. You could feel the tension in the room. Finally, after the visitor had referred for the sixth time to "the Gospel," a hand went up towards the back of the small sea of faded clerical shirts and argyll socks. "Just exactly what do you mean, Bishop, by 'the Gospel'?" The bishop shot back, "I mean this: Christ died for our sins."

This writer was only a seminarian at the time, but the bishop's answer ripped through me like a razor! "Christ died for our sins." I sensed myself diagnosed, cleanly, surgically, cleansingly. No pretend: I needed a savior and that was Christ.

There is something freeing about an accurate diagnosis. Terminal patients will sometimes say that they can live with the truth. What they cannot live with is uncertainty and equivocation.

Can you connect with the insight here, that for our sins we deserve to be punished? Moreover, that the grace, or unmerited love of God, can so provide forgiveness that the "discomfort" of being pinned down like a butterfly can be relieved?

This is the good news of guilt brought to light and guilt forgiven: in other words, news of lasting comfort.

The Fifth Sunday in Lent

THE COLLECT

e beseech thee, almighty God, mercifully to look upon thy people; that by thy great goodness they may be governed and preserved evermore, both in body and soul; through Jesus Christ our Lord.

HISTORY

The common title "Passion Sunday" has some medieval precedent, but the term "Passiontide" originated within the Church of England during the late nineteenth century.

The Collect is from the Gregorian Sacramentary. The original Latin *"familia"* is here rendered "people" ("household").

MEDITATION

Why do we need to be governed? Because we need to be preserved.

Such is the reasoning of the Collect. The thought process is as follows: Without some restraint or order, the human situation moves irresistibly towards chaos: party out of bounds! God's government of the world, and God's government of the self, are parallel. Sin, the even distribution of human nature, erupts chronically and constantly. Sin needs to be kept in bounds.

Only with sin restrained, will the self, let alone the plural selves that make up society, find itself preserved. The world descends to chaos, goes this argument, when the evil impulse is not checked. The argument is unavoidably true. It is empirically verifiable.

The question now becomes, How is sin checked? How is human nature governed? Is it governed by external restraint imposed, or is it governed by internal restraint engendered? To put it another way, are we ruled in God's economy by the Law (i.e., external or un-free restraint) or by Grace (i.e., internal or free restraint)?

The Prayer Book answers the question decisively. We are ruled "by thy great goodness." It could have said, "by thy massive judgment," or "by thy massive deterrence through the threat of punishment." But it does not say that.

Rather, we pray to God that by God's great goodness we may be governed and preserved evermore. The root of sin's abeyance is the goodness of God. We become better from the effects of mercy, not from the effects of judgment. Or was Charles Dickens wrong? And Victor Hugo?

The Sunday next before Easter

THE COLLECT

Almighty and everlasting God, which of thy tender love toward man, hast sent our Savior Jesus Christ, to take upon him our flesh, and to suffer death upon the cross, that all mankind should follow the example of his great humility; mercifully grant that we both follow the example of his patience, and be made partakers of his resurrection; through the same Jesus Christ our lord.

HISTORY

This Sunday is commonly (but not officially) called Palm Sunday from the old practice of bearing palms (often willows in England) in commemoration of Our Lord's triumphal entry into Jerusalem. The Collect, which emphasizes that there is no Crown without the Cross, is from the Sacramentary of Gelasius.

MEDITATION

It helps to make these prayers count for us when we locate the verbs. It helps to locate the petition, which is to say what is being asked. Sometimes a prayer, like King Solomon's in I Chronicles 29 or the Prophet Nehemiah's in his first chapter or Jeremiah's in the middle of his chapter 32, takes awhile to get started. Sometimes the Collect surrounds God with pertinent adjectives and descriptive clauses (i.e., the acknowledgement). But if you look, and keep looking, there is always eventually a verb, and almost always eventually an object.

Here, on the Sunday of Holy Week, which we know today as Palm Sunday, the verb is "grant." The object is dual: that we would "follow the example of his patience" and that we would "be made partakers of his resurrection." The intention is first that we would become more like Christ, in particular in His humble bearing of His life's work during this week. Here is the element of obedient following which is captured classically in Thomas à Kempis' *The Imitation of Christ*.

The intention is, second, that we would so get through the shadows of this life that we would make it to the promised land, the life yonder. Here we can refer to John Ford's not-often-enough-seen motion picture *Wagonmaster* (1950). There, at the conclusion, after the wagon train has made it through to the goal, after armies of struggle and setback and catastrophe, the pioneers stand and sing, "All is well."

In sum, we ask at the start of our most important week to be granted both perseverance in His way and fulfillment of His achievement. This is Holy Week's prayer, from His entry into the city to His empty tomb Easter morning.

45

On Good Friday

THE FIRST COLLECT
(at Matins)

Almighty God, we beseech thee graciously to behold this thy family, for the which our lord Jesus Christ was contented to be betrayed, and given up into the hands of wicked men, and to suffer death upon the cross: who liveth and reigneth, &c.

HISTORY

The term Good Friday originated in medieval England. It refers to the great blessings conferred upon mankind by the sacrifice of Christ.

In the Sarum liturgy this was a post-communion Collect for Wednesday in Holy Week, linking to the Gospel (St. Mark 14:10f.) of Our Lord's betrayal.

MEDITATION

The most important day of the year for Christians is Easter Day. But not in isolation! Rather, the most important day for Christians is Easter Day in the light of Good Friday. If Good Friday took away the "sting of death" (I Corinthians 15:56), which is the Law (i.e., guilt for the things done and the things left undone), Good Friday is nevertheless ratified by Easter. The death would have been noble in a human sense, but entirely unfruitful in an enduring sense if Christ had not overcome death. There would be no abiding forgiveness of sins if the instrument of that forgiveness, the man-God Jesus Christ (Kierkegaard's phrase), had not returned to abide — had He not returned to life. We emphasize the unbreakable bond between the dying on Good Friday and the raising on Easter.

Here, in the first Collect for Good Friday, the prayer is disarming. It is for just one thing: for God "graciously to behold this thy family." Look on us! Draw your attention to us as we rehearse this drama in two acts, the memory and vivid power of two indispensable acts which took place on our behalf. Help us, O God, to enter into this.

The prayer is preparatory. We are about to do something that is truly serious. There is nothing more important for human beings to commit to than to make our own these two events. This is to take your hat off for, this is to salute for, this is to kneel for, or stand up for, or do anything that says, "I am totally fixed on this one thing."

So the best (two) days of our lives, Good Friday and Easter, count. Watch us, O Lord, and bless us as we enter the days that changed the world.

On Good Friday

THE FIRST COLLECT
(At the Communion)

lmighty and everlasting God, by whose spirit the whole body of the Church is governed and sanctified; receive our supplications and prayers, which we offer before thee for all estates of men in thy holy congregation, that every member of the same, in his vocation and ministry, may truly and godly serve thee; through our Lord Jesus Christ.

THE SECOND COLLECT
(At the Communion)

erciful God, who hast made all men, and hatest nothing that thou has made, nor wouldest the death of a sinner, but rather that he should be converted and live; have mercy upon all Jews, Turks, Infidels and heretics, and take from them all ignorance, hardness of heart, and contempt of thy word: and so fetch them home, blessed Lord, to thy flock, that they may be saved among the remnant of the true Israelites, and be made one fold under one shepherd, Jesus Christ our Lord; who liveth and reigneth, &c.

HISTORY

These two Collects "at the Communion" would have been used in the Ante-Communion service on Good Friday. Medieval usage had permitted only the "Mass of the Pre-Sanctified." This service was eliminated by our Reformers.

The first of these Collects is one of a series of solemn prayers in the Roman Catholic rite for Good Friday expanded to include all members of the Church. The second, composed at the Reformation, is based on Ezekiel 18:23, 33:11 and St. John 10:16. The Jews believe in God, but reject Christ. The Mohammedans believe in God and honor Christ, but do not yield Him divine honor. Infidels are those who do not believe the basic doctrines of Christianity. Heretics are Christians who maintain religious opinions contrary to the teachings of the Church. This prayer is more a call to missionary work than a statement of judgment.

MEDITATION

These two Collects comprise a dialogue between a proper inwardness on the part of the Christian Church and a dedicated outwardness in respect to the spiritual needs of the world.

The first Collect asks that all Christians be enabled to serve God in whatever situation they are in. Hold it! The Collect asks *merely?* The request is for godly living. This prayer on Good Friday asks God to order us in the right way. It is a panoramic request. What it means for you and me is that we be enabled to see our concrete situation as God's intended avenue for us to perform the works of love. Our actual situation, so goes the logic of the Collect, is not the road wrongly traveled or the thwartedness of a proper path blocked and detoured. Rather, the pathway on which we find ourselves, our here and now, is the ready place for our life's God-intended "vocation and ministry." The premise is of a God who knows what He is doing with our life. Is that admissible to you, as you observe in hindsight your own "road less traveled"?

The second Collect for Good Friday points us on to two further insights. The first insight is that God "hatest nothing that (He) has made." God created us and no matter how fallen away from grace we actually are, His eye is on the sparrow. He resolved after Noah's Flood (Genesis 9:8-17) never again to destroy the earth: neither the sons of Adam nor the daughters of Eve (C. S. Lewis). No matter how far gone we are (Article IX of the Thirty-Nine Articles), He does not hate us. This is because He made us. Thus there is always hope for us "at all times and in all places."

Moreover, we are invited here to pray for "all Jews, Turks (i.e., Muslims), Infidels and heretics . . . that they may be saved among the remnant of the true Israelites." The conviction is that the non-Christian needs converting. The claim of Christ's Lordship, to use the Pauline phrase, is absolute and universal. Whether this claim of Christianity on the whole world sits well with contemporary thinking or not, the claim is asserted and made specific within Cranmer's Collect. Can you swallow this? It stands written.

Easter Day

THE COLLECT AT THE FIRST COMMUNION

lmighty God, which through thy only begotten son Jesus Christ hast overcome death, and opened unto us the gate of everlasting life; we humbly beseech thee, that, as by thy special grace, preventing us, thou dost put in our minds good desires, so by thy continual help we may bring the same to good effect; through Jesus Christ our Lord who liveth and reigneth, &c.

HISTORY

The first part of our Easter Collect comes from the Sacramentary of Gelasius, altered to offset the Pelagian teaching that it is possible to do God's will without the assistance of divine grace (Article X of the Articles of Religion). Stephens-Hodge notes that "this heresy is by no means extinct."

MEDITATION

The Collect proclaims the New Covenant! The Old Covenant said that a good man is defined by his deeds (St. Matthew 5:21-43). The New Covenant says that a good man is defined by his motives (St. Matthew 5:22-48). The New Covenant observes and ratifies the truth that good fruit springs only from a good root.

So here, a seemingly anticlimactic concentration — on Easter Day, for heaven's sake! — upon good deeds is absolutely proper. For it is because "Jesus Christ hast overcome death," that He is still, now and in the present moment, working in us. His work is to go before us (i.e., "prevent us" in Cranmer's idiom), to instill in us "good desires," and to help bring such desires to fruition in life. Were it not for the Resurrection, God would be dead, or still dead, and certainly dead for purposes of practical application in our lives. But because He lives, He is with us yet. He is the current inspirer of loving intentions. Loving intentions are the point of origin for loving deeds.

This is Easter understood not so much as cosmic victory (as in the Orthodox tradition), but Easter as Enabler of the Ethical. The point of the Gospel is always to enable the ethical, or better, to create the seed of love that flowers in the ethical, which is the good life.

The First Sunday after Easter

THE COLLECT

Almighty father, which hast given thy only son to die for our sins, and to rise again for our justification; Grant us so to put away the leaven of malice and wickedness, that we may always serve thee in pureness of living and truth; through Jesus Christ our Lord.

HISTORY

This actually is the Collect for the "second Communion" on Easter Day, repeated on "Low Sunday." It is an original composition by Archbishop Cranmer for the 1549 Prayer Book. The Collect was lost when a second celebration was swept away in the 1552 Prayer Book. In 1662 Bishop Wren suggested restoring it for use on the First Sunday after Easter.

The origin of the popular English designation "Low Sunday" is supposed by some to reflect its contrast with the great Feast with which the Octave opened. Alternatively, it may be a corruption of *Laudes,* the first word of the pre-Reformation sequence, *Laudes Salvatori voce modulemer supplici.*

MEDITATION

What is the "leaven of malice and wickedness" which the Collect bids us put away? The impact of the Collect depends on our understanding what this leaven is.

"Leaven" refers to teaching (St. Matthew 16:11; St. Luke 12:1). Leaven is used in the Gospels to denote the teaching of the Pharisees and Sadducees, which is specified further, in Luke's Gospel, as being hypocrisy. The idea is that the Pharisees and Sadducees teach an observance of God's Law which so depends on external performance, in contrast to internal or heartfelt response, that it produces hypocrisy. So much emphasis is placed by their teaching on rectitude, that the motives and intentions inside the person come to be of less weight than the actual doing of the things as observed from the outside.

The problem with this, and the reason why Jesus excoriates it as producing "whited sepulchers," which outside are nice enough to look at but inside are full of dead men's bones (St. Matthew 23:27), is that performance on its own terms can easily conceal a tawdry bag of mixed motives. The results of hypocrisy include *malice* (i.e., active resentment and envy) and *wickedness* (i.e., immorality, conspiracy, and active evil hidden).

Now we can understand why the Collect focuses on the Lord who rose again "for our justification." In order to avoid the "leaven" or teaching of Pharisaism, which clocks in the deed rather than the "will for the deed," we have to know that our status before God has been secured previously. We do not require justification before other people, or self-justification, or even justification before God on the basis of any outward standard. God has justified us by placing us in a new sphere of unimpeachable regard. This He has done by virtue of the death and resurrection of Christ. Therefore, we, being justified, do not require the imperative "Just Do It." Christ has done it.

The Collect for Easter I, pure Thomas Cranmer in its formation, arrangement, and placement, draws profoundly on St. Paul's linking of our *justification* with Christ's *resurrection* in Romans 4:25. If the prayer does nothing more than send us back to that verse, it has done its job well.

The Second Sunday after Easter

THE COLLECT

lmighty God, which hast given thy holy son to be unto us, both a sacrifice for sin, and also an example of Godly life; Give us the grace that we may always most thankfully receive that his inestimable benefit, and also daily endeavor ourselves to follow the blessed steps of his most holy life.

HISTORY

This Sunday is popularly called "Good Shepherd Sunday" from the theme which is common to the Epistle (I St. Peter 2:19) and the Gospel (St. John 10:11) for the day. The Collect likewise has special reference to the duties of pastors of Christian flocks. In sixteenth-century English, "endeavor" is used as a reflexive verb. No emphasis is placed on the pronoun, for we "ourselves" can accomplish nothing without the prevenient grace of God. This Collect was first composed for the 1549 Prayer Book.

MEDITATION

I once overheard a clergyman taking a churchgoing family hotly to task for "the practical atheism in which you all live." The phrase chilled me. It seemed so true for so many: *practical* atheism in the midst of sincere but abstracted belief.

That phrase, "the practical atheism in which you all live," helps us understand this Collect, which is a conscious deterrent to "practical Pelagianism." Practical Pelagianism is any way of living by which responsibility for the willing and doing of the right thing is yours. The ball is in your court, really and actually, rather than that of the unseen God. You may pray to God, even for specific assistance, but you act as though it were up to you.

There was a vicar friend in England widely admired for his piety and zeal. Every morning he would, in the context of his early quiet time, "commend my day to the Lord." Then full steam ahead: He was off and running. He believed in God, but he acted like a thoroughgoing Pelagian. Pelagianism, by the way, is the teaching named for a fifth-century British monk, Pelagius. It is the formal name for a Christian heresy — we believe it to be a universal heresy — that human beings can, with just a little help from God, accomplish their own salvation, or at least achieve their personal worth or worthwhileness.

The Collect for the Second Sunday after Easter parries Pelagianism. Yes, it invites us to follow Christ. Yes, it sets out Christ as the way-shower and exemplar of the human race. But it beds the exemplary character of Christ's life in his "sacrifice for sin" and "his inestimable benefit" (i.e., for us). In theological language, we could say that the Collect invokes the Atonement as the foundation of our living out concretely a Christ-like life.

In everyday terms, belovedness precedes loving. Is this not true in secure human relationships? Cranmer sees it as true in the prime relationship.

The Third Sunday after Easter

THE COLLECT

Almighty God, which showest to all men that be in error the light of thy truth, to the intent that they may return into the way of righteousness; Grant unto all them that be admitted into the fellowship of Christ's religion, that they may eschew those things that be contrary to their profession, and follow all such things as be agreeable to the same; through our Lord Jesus Christ.

HISTORY

This Collect is from the Sacramentary of Leo I and is one of the oldest in the Prayer Book. The petition reflects the fact that Easter is a principal time for baptism, thus the reference to "all them that be admitted into the fellowship of Christ's religion" (Lat. *qui Christiana professione censentor* — who are enrolled as Christians by profession).

MEDITATION

Is there a tangible relation in your life between what you believe and the way you act? It is an easy question to ask. But is there any organic, substantial, or material relation between what you believe and the way you live? Not a theoretical relationship (as in "I think it exists") or even an ideal relationship (as in "I hope it exists"), but rather an actual relationship (as in "it does exist, plainly and visibly"). Is there an empirical connection between "the truth" and your life? Do others see such a connection in you?

The Collect for the Third Sunday after Easter draws its power from the relation it represents between "the light of thy truth" and "the way of righteousness." We might have expected the Collect to posit God's showing forth His light to all "that be in error," to the intent that we would return to His truth. But no! The intent of our receiving His light is, in Prayer Book logic, that we return to "the way of righteousness." Truth creates right doing!

How can this be so? Truth here must be something potent in practice. It must be more than an abstraction. It must be more than principles or correct thinking. It is in fact right relationship. It is fellowship with God, to use the Collect's phrase. Truth enables relationship. The link between truth and relationship is the truth about ourselves in the light of the truth about God. When we are truly known, particularly in the darkness and shadows of our lives, by a Love which does not reject, we are cemented to God. To be known in truth and at the same time loved is the *coup de grâce* to our retreat from relationship.

If what you believe is God's truth (grace) and your truth (the way you really are), the fruit of your belief will be works of righteousness and "all such things as be agreeable to the same." The relation between what you believe and what you do will be of cement, or better, of steel.

The Fourth Sunday after Easter

THE COLLECT

lmighty God, which dost make the minds of all faithful men to be of one will; grant unto thy people, that they may love the thing, which thou commandest, and desire, that which thou dost promise; that among the sundry and manifold changes of the world, our hearts may surely there be fixed, where true joys are to be found; through Christ our Lord.

HISTORY

This Collect from the Sacramentary of Gelasius is a prayer for Church unity. The revisers of 1662 changed the invocation thus: "O Almighty God, who alone canst order the unruly wills and affection of sinful men," reflecting the preceding years of civil strife and the Commonwealth's suppression of the Church of England, its episcopacy, and its Prayer Book.

58

MEDITATION

This Collect is one of the high points of Anglican theology, a masterpiece of pure, perfect, prayed theology.

The prayer bids us love that which we are required to do. The vision is for people to obey God's commandment not out of constraint, nor even out of a sense of duty, but rather out of spontaneous desire. What a revolutionary idea! For the *I ought* to be the same thing as the *I want*.

Are we not more typically in conflict? Romans 7 describes the human predicament of our not being able to do what we ought to do. We actually do what we know we ought not to do! (v. 19). St. Paul sees the human condition as one of experienced wretchedness (v. 24), because the Law of God is unable to be fulfilled by conflicted human nature.

The Apostle resolves this universal conflict by affirming that the forgiveness of God (8:1) makes it possible for the human being to begin willing *from the heart* what is right to do in agreement with God's will. The title of a film by Francis Ford Coppola entitled *One from the Heart* (1982) catches the wave of Christian ethics. Right doing comes from the inward will of a person, not from outward demands upon that person.

The Prayer Book caught the same wave in 1549. It understood the revolutionary change in the ethical life when it moves from constraint to desire. To live from love and not from obligation is to exist in the precise place where "true joys are to be found."

Ask yourself, what percentage of your actions are performed from some claim of "ought"? What percentage are performed from some quality of "I want"? Do the "I ought" and the "I want" ever conjoin? When? It "doesn't get any better than this" in life: to love the thing "which thou commandest." It is paradise on earth.

The Fifth Sunday after Easter

THE COLLECT

ord from whom all good things do come; grant us, thy humble servants, that by thy holy inspiration we may think those things that be good, and by thy merciful guiding may perform the same; through our Lord Jesus Christ.

HISTORY

This Gelasian Collect's opening phrase is linked with the Epistle for the previous Sunday, "Every good and perfect gift is from above" (James 1:17). Later, this Sunday would be known as "Rogation Sunday" for the three Rogation Days which follow. The appropriateness of this Collect to Rogation ("asking") is purely coincidental. At Rogation we ask God's blessings on the crops and labors of our hands.

MEDITATION

We are on the same ground here as with the previous Collect. The focus is on human inwardness ("that . . . we may think those things that be good") as prior to and causative of human outward action (that we "may perform the same").

Aristotle had written in the *Nicomachean Ethics* (1103b 1f.) that if a man performs those things that are good, he thereby becomes good. This teaching, that good deeds create moral goodness in a person, permeated late medieval thought and culture. It had thoroughly convinced the Christian Church. It had been the air breathed by every one of the English Reformers from their earliest training to be priests. They were all ordained priests of the Roman Church before they became our blessed Reformers.

The Aristotelian teaching about how a man becomes good had failed them! It had failed them because they had observed in experience that it did not work. Also they read in the New Testament a wholly different understanding of the human situation. In the Gospels and Epistles, they saw that a human being must first discover himself to be good because God has forgiven him and therefore declared him good, before he is able to do good deeds. Cranmer and his Cambridge University colleagues checked *Aristotle's* idea against what they read in *St. Paul.* Aristotle had to go!

In fact, Hans Holbein the Younger, who became court artist to Henry VIII during the early years of Cranmer's reform, created a woodcut in which Aristotle was depicted as fleeing before the shining candle of the Gospel.

In Cranmer's Collect for the Fifth Sunday after Easter, Aristotle and his whole concept of virtue is in roaring and full-scale flight from the Truth.

The Ascension Day

THE COLLECT

rant we beseech thee, almighty god, that like as we do believe thy only begotten son our lord to have ascended into the heavens; so we may also in heart and mind thither ascend, and with him continually dwell.

HISTORY

This great festival, so neglected in our day, was intended by Archbishop Cranmer to be observed with special honor. Since it is given its own Proper Psalms, Proper Lessons, Collect, Epistle, Gospel, and Proper Preface, it ranks with Christmas, Easter Day, and Whitsunday. The Collect is from the Sacramentary of Gregory, but the leading thought is from the Sacramentary of Gelasius. Cranmer used "our Lord" in place of "our Redeemer" and added "heart" to "mind." The dating of the feast forty days after Easter is based on Acts 1:3.

MEDITATION

This prayer for Christ's Ascension (Acts 1:9) connects His absence with our present. The prayer affirms that we can even now be with Christ in "heart and mind." The biblical reference is to that astounding verse, Ephesians 2:6.

What can this possibly mean in real terms, that we may in the present tense "dwell" with Christ, emotionally "in heart" and intellectually "in mind"? The idea is that Christians are such solid participants in the life of Christ on earth, that we are also simultaneously relating to Him in His heavenly session. The "heavenly session" is what our forebears called the seatedness of Christ at God's right hand, while the "Church militant" (i.e., we) remain physically, geographically separated from Him.

This Collect borders on a mysticism that the Reformers generally eschewed. The Collect reveals at the same time their conscious intention to be true to the whole of Scripture. We could even say that a Collect like this one, so odd to make sense of in rational terms, is a reminder to Christians that not so much *sola scriptura,* as rather *tota scriptura* is the best way to proceed with the Bible.

Ephesians 2:6 is there for a purpose. It exalts the human being "who is in Christ" to a sphere of connectedness with God in the now which lies beyond rational explanation.

The Collect for the Ascension of Christ implores us to travel with Him, through the veil, in our prayers of the heart and our meditations of the mind. This is a Christianity which is not so much high-flying as it is high-minded.

The Sunday after the Ascension

THE COLLECT

O God, the king of glory, which hast exalted thine only son Jesus Christ, with great triumph unto thy kingdom in heaven; we beseech thee, leave us not comfortless; but send us thine holy ghost to comfort us, and exalt us unto the same place whither our savior Christ is gone before; who liveth and reigneth &c.

HISTORY

The pre-Reformation Sarum Collect for this Sunday contained no seasonal reference. It was replaced by Cranmer with an original composition for the 1549 Prayer Book. It is based on an antiphon which for many years had been sung at Vespers on Ascension Day, which ran "O King of Glory, Lord of Hosts, who today didst ascend in triumph far above all heavens, do not leave us orphans. . . ." Tradition holds that it was sung by the Venerable Bede on his deathbed.

MEDITATION

The theme of Christ's Ascension into heaven is probed here a second time, but in a different way.

The first part of the petition is that we be not left comfortless in the face of Christ's physical absence. There is a heart-rending note sounded here: Don't leave me alone! I had you once, I saw you and touched you. I need you, but now you're gone. What shall I do? Do you hear me saying it?: Why did you leave me? I am without comfort, like Rachel weeping for her children (St. Matthew 2:18; Jeremiah 31:15).

The pathos of the Ascension, somewhat muted in the earlier Collect for Ascension Day itself, is now fully acknowledged. Home alone. Alone again.

The difference, however, is that the prayer implores God, on the basis of St. John 14, to send the Holy Spirit to give us that comfort which the world cannot give. We are not in fact alone. The personal presence of God was promised by Jesus. This prayer counts on it.

And not only shall the Spirit of God provide that comfort so needed within the vale of tears that is life (honestly represented), but the Spirit will "exalt us" ultimately yonder, over Jordan, over the river of death, to the place where Christ has gone before.

The themes of the Collect are absence, solitude, accompaniment, and passage to the Kingdom of Light — right through to the end, and beyond "the end."

Whitsunday

THE COLLECT

od, which as upon this day hast taught the hearts of thy faithful people, by the sending to them the light of thy holy spirit; grant us by the same spirit to have a right judgment in all things; and evermore to rejoice in his holy comfort; through the merits of Christ Jesus our savior; who liveth and reigneth with thee, in the unity of the same spirit, one God, world without end.

HISTORY

The Christian festival of Whitsunday parallels the Jewish festival of Pentecost, as the Christian Easter corresponds to Passover. As the Hebrew Pentecost commemorates the giving of the Law on Mt. Sinai and is also a time of harvest thanksgiving, so the Church celebrates the coming of the Holy Spirit and the Church's first harvest of souls.

Cranmer added the words *in all things, evermore,* and *holy* to this prayer from the Gregorian Sacramentary.

The English name of the Feast is a shortening of "White Sunday," referring to the white garments worn by the newly baptized on this day. The weather was warmer in England than at Easter and more baptisms took place at this later season.

MEDITATION

*"If I do not go away, the Comforter will not come to you; but
if I go, I will send him to you."*

St. John 16:7

*Here the new beginning of life in the Holy Spirit is directly
linked with the mystery of redemption. Through the force of
his surrender of himself to death on the cross, Christ sends the
Spirit of life. That is the revelation of love in the pain of God,
which makes new life for sinners and the dying possible. . . . A
true theology of the cross is Pentecost theology, and Christian
Pentecost theology is a theology of the cross.*

Jürgen Moltmann, *The Source of Life,* 1997, p. 17.

The gift of God's presence, so comforting to the abandoned human
heart, the heart left, tangibly, by Christ at the moment of His disap-
pearance on Ascension Day, is linked in the above quotation to the
crucifixion. The death of Christ is the "revelation of love in the pain
of God." When Christ dies, then rises, but then departs again, the
enormous abyss of human vulnerability is opened up as darkly and
fathomlessly as possible. We need the Comforter. We need the reas-
surance of God come back. We need Pentecost.

The Prayer Book Collect for Whitsunday ("Pentecost" in Greek)
ties the coming of the comforting Spirit to the death of the Son. This
is because the gift of the Holy Spirit is given "through the merits of
Jesus Christ our savior." It is because of the sacrifice of God in
Christ, which wiped away guilt but only at the cost of eliminating
forever Christ's earthly presence among us, that the disciples were
left alone. God must respond to their comfortlessness.

Similarly, to be gracious, which we know He is, God must respond to our dereliction and forlornness. The joy you and I receive
from the sent Spirit's "holy comfort" is the joy of receiving, back
from the dead, One upon whom our whole health depends.

Trinity Sunday

THE COLLECT

lmighty and everlasting God, which hast given unto us thy servants grace by the confession of a true faith to acknowledge the glory of the eternal trinity, and in the power of the divine majesty to worship the unity: we beseech thee, that through the steadfastness of this faith, we may ever more be defended from all adversity, which livest and reignest, one God, world without end.

HISTORY

The first half of the Christian year is used to set forth the great doctrines of the Christian religion ("the acts our great Redeemer wrought"). The second half teaches us practical duties, our response to what God has accomplished for us in Christ. Neither is complete without the other. Trinity Sunday links the two halves together.

MEDITATION

Almost no one has ever plumbed the depths of the Trinity in a short and concise manner, or, better, in an understandable manner. The usual and also the historic definition of the Trinity is this: The Three in One, One God in Three Persons. Beyond that, it gets, to put it mildly, complex.

But the Prayer Book comes close, in the Collect for Trinity Sunday. It catches the concept deftly and briefly, but also ties it in, as always, to real life.

The prayer captures the concept within two infinitives: "to acknowledge the glory of the eternal trinity" and "in the power of the divine majesty to worship the unity." This is the idea that God is One, which was always taught within Judaism and, later, by Islam. But it is also the idea that the One God has revealed Himself in severalness, in a divine family.

The pre-Socratic philosopher Parmenides talked about the one and the many, both as opposites and as unity. The history of God's revelation in the Bible ratified this thinking. Cranmer codified it within the language of prayer: "trinity," "majesty," and "unity." But there is more to it than that.

The Collect suggests that if we are clear about God's self-revelation as Trinity ("through the steadfastness of this faith"), we may "ever more be defended from all adversity." If we know the truth about God, it will defend us. The idea is that ideas matter. Skewed ideas will get us into trouble. Right ideas will aid us and defend us.

A key source for this bond affirmed between "the steadfastness of faith" and our defense from all adversity is the passage in Ephesians 5 concerning the armor of God. "Therefore take the whole armor of God, that you may be able to withstand in the evil day, and having done all, to stand. Stand therefore, having girded your loins with truth . . ." (vv. 13-14). To put it crisply, truth discerns the lie, and the lie is that the devil can overpower God. But he cannot. The Triune God is an impenetrable fortress around us.

The First Sunday after Trinity

THE COLLECT

O od, the strength of all them that trust in thee, mercifully accept our prayers; and because the weakness of our mortal nature can do no good thing without thee, grant us the help of thy grace, that in keeping of thy commandments we may please thee, both in will and deed; through Jesus Christ our lord.

HISTORY

The Book of Common Prayer follows the Sarum Missal in naming the remaining Sundays of the Church Year as "Sundays after Trinity." The Church of Rome in 1570 officially directed that these be called "Sundays after Pentecost."

Archbishop Cranmer translated this Collect from the Gregorian Sacramentary, substituting only "trust" for "hope."

MEDITATION

A prayer is prayed because the one praying it is in contact with his need. The need from which this Collect arises is "the weakness of our mortal nature" which "can do no good thing without thee."

Note three key words: One, *weakness,* for we do not possess the strength to do what is right. Our foundations lack the grounding to support ethical humane living. Two, *mortal,* for we are coursing towards the universal terminus of physical death. Even if we were not weak, even if we were somehow strong in ourselves, the sun would set over our achievements, forever. Three, *no good thing,* a phrase that excludes even the possibility of a decent action undertaken without the aid of God's grace. "No good thing" declares the nullification of unaided human potential to accomplish good.

The Collect is a bitter pill. It lays out our hope of self-improvement like the boxer who offers no quarter. No wonder the "modern mind" is uneasy with what the mystery writer P. D. James calls "the Cranmerian protestantism" of the Prayer Book. It offers to modernism absolutely nothing, neither a fish nor an egg.

On the other hand, the prayer offers everything.

What does it actually ask? "Grant us the help of thy grace." The negativity concerning the human condition is good news if it is transformed into a passionate and decided cry for help from the outside. The prayer holds out the promise that with the help of the prior love and grace of Christ, we may begin to do right (the "keeping of thy commandments"). Moreover, doing right holds out the greater promise of pleasing God. Here we have gone from total negation of the possibility of measuring up to total optimism: that God can be pleased with us both as we are within (i.e., "in will") and as we are without (i.e., "in deed"). To please the One with whom we have to do both inwardly and outwardly — that is to be very little short of divinized ourselves; better, made worthy of living with God.

No wonder Pascal never tired of saying that the Christian was both the world's most wretched person, absolutely needy; and the world's grandee, absolutely guaranteed in love and status.

The Second Sunday after Trinity

THE COLLECT

ord, make us to have a perpetual fear and love of thy holy name: for thou never failest to help and govern them whom thou dost bring up in thy steadfast love. Grant this, &c.

HISTORY

This Collect, from the Gelasian Sacramentary, was translated into English (closely following the Latin) for the 1549 Prayer Book but, as Massey Shepherd points out, Cranmer failed to convey the illuminating metaphor of the original, which likened God's help to that of a pilot or helmsman. We fear the pilot because he alone can bring us to safety; we love him because he does not abandon us. It is this "godly fear" of which the hymnwriter says:

Fear him, ye saints, and you will then
    Have nothing else to fear.

The revisers of the 1662 Prayer Book rearranged and expanded several clauses.

MEDITATION

The Collect puts us face to face with two apparent contradictions in the life of faith.

The first apparent contradiction is that which exists between "fear" of God and "love" of God. It brings to mind the Robert Mitchum character in *The Night of the Hunter* (1955). That classic Hollywood type, the psychopathic preacher, had the word "H•A•T•E" written on the four knuckles of one hand and the word "L•O•V•E" written on the other. Could the two be true of the same man? Similarly, how could we both fear and love God at the same time?

We fear Him because He has the entire authority over us of life and death (St. Matthew 10:28; Hebrews 10:30-31). God is by definition our Creator and by historical intervention our Redeemer. We owe Him everything. Jonathan Edwards was right: "It is a fearful thing to fall into the hands of the living God!" There is nothing unsavory or embarrassing about this. It is a truth of life. Just sit with someone who has just heard the words of a terminal diagnosis. It may be a cleansing moment, even a moment shot through with love and gratitude. But it is a moment of holy fear.

Yet we *love* Him, also. We love Him because His "new best name is love" (Charles Wesley). This is because God is known to us as "brother of our Flesh, and of our Bone" (also Wesley), in other words, as Jesus who was one of us. So it is not exactly true that we both fear God and love Him concurrently, but rather that our proper fear is comprehended and subsumed under the final word of love.

The second apparent contradiction in the Collect stems from an experienced enigma of human life. Can we honestly argue with this prayer that "thou never failest to help and govern them whom thou dost bring up in thy steadfast love"? Could we not rather point to exceptions? He sure failed me there; or when she died, I honestly thought to myself, God has let me down. Nevertheless, the words of the Collect are inescapable: He never fails us, period. Is this an affirmation you can make? Or perhaps in hindsight?

Isaac Watts said it tersely, and awesomely:

If smiling Mercy crown our lives
Its praises shall be spread,
And we'll adore the Justice too
That strikes our comforts dead.

The Third Sunday after Trinity

THE COLLECT

ord, we beseech thee mercifully to hear us, and unto whom thou hast given a hearty desire to pray; grant that by thy mighty aid we may be defended; through Jesus Christ our Lord.

HISTORY

This Collect from the Sacramentary of Gregory was taken into the Sarum Missal and from there to the 1549 Prayer Book. The revisers in 1662 added a final clause, "and comforted in all dangers and adversities."

MEDITATION

There is one assumption that all the Collects carry. In this one, the Collect for the Third Sunday after Trinity, that assumption is explicit. It is the assumption that prayers exist because we desire to pray them! "Lord . . . hear us . . . unto whom thou hast given a hearty desire to pray."

Would you even be reading this book, or biting it off one Collect at a time, if you did not feel a "hearty desire to pray"? All this material, all this work of compiling, translating, creating, editing, and rewriting which Cranmer undertook in order to present the Prayer Book for "common" use: it all assumes that prayer is a good, desirable thing. We wish to talk to God. We wish to present our concerns and worries, our Sisyphean burdens and our most treasured, fragile hopes to God.

Yet we fail to do this. It is striking how many important problems we fail to put into words before God. It is startling how often the biggest troubles we have are the last ones to find expression in our praying. That is probably because we have given up hope of intervention or transformation in the really vexing areas. In any event, take inventory. Which of your life's problems at this moment is not a conscious part of your prayers? Ever?

It is no wonder that this concise Collect understands that the desire to pray is the gift of God. The desire to pray should not be assumed, in fact, at all. Remember the old hymn:

> O what peace we often forfeit,
>   O what needless pain we bear,
> All because we do not carry
>   Ev'rything to God in prayer!

(*The Hymnal 1940*, No. 422)

75

The Fourth Sunday after Trinity

THE COLLECT

God the protector of all that trust in thee, without whom nothing is strong, nothing is holy; increase and multiply upon us thy mercy; that thou being our ruler and guide, we may so pass through things temporal, that we finally lose not the things eternal: Grant this heavenly father, for Jesus Christ's sake our Lord.

HISTORY

Again a translation from the Gregorian Sacramentary, but here the English version is preferable: "things temporal" (Latin *bona temporalia* — "the good things of time"). We are in danger not only from temporal adversity, but also from temporal prosperity.

MEDITATION

This is one of the most famous and hence most frequently memorized Collects from the Prayer Book. It is a masterpiece of spare, affecting English rhetoric.

It contains, however, one shocking request, or rather a request that hinges on a shocking thought. The request is that "we may so pass through things temporal, that we finally lose not the things eternal." The shocking thought is that we actually could lose those things, those lasting things, such as eternal life, enduring love, and companionship with God in heaven. The disquieting thought is that eternity, specifically our eternity, cannot be taken for granted, that our hold on it is fragile.

How shall we understand this? One way is to look back on your life up to this point. Do you ever see your life, in hindsight, at least, if not during the events when they actually happened, as an obstacle course? There was this to be overcome; there was that curve ball; there was this temptation, which got you; there was that temptation, which somehow you resisted; there was this particular timing of a death in your family; there was that particular life's partner, or almost life's partner, who just about wrecked you for good; and so forth and so on. Someone observed once, about a marriage of many years, "The trouble was, it ended badly. What should have ended well, didn't. And the ending cast a shadow over everything, even the good things which had preceded it." Bad luck? Destiny?

It certainly is possible, humanly speaking, to "so pass through things temporal" that you achieve the shorehold of Jordan, i.e., the period before death, feeling you have lost the abiding things — like belovedness, for example. Life could harden you, or embitter you even, to the point that you arrived at the end wishing you had given back your original ticket of admission! That image is from *The Brothers Karamazov*.

The Collect understands this. The Collect comprehends our vulnerability to loss, even the loss of everything. What is *Citizen Kane* about if it is not about a man who has lost the one thing eternal, which is love? So we pray, earnestly, to be held by God, in the course of this life, right through its passages, right through its adolescence, its adulthood, its mid-life and old age, right through and on to Jordan's verge.

The Fifth Sunday after Trinity

THE COLLECT

 rant Lord, we beseech thee, that the course of this world may be so peaceably ordered by thy governance, that thy congregation may joyfully serve thee in all godly quietness; through Jesus Christ our Lord.

HISTORY

This Collect is found in the Sacramentaries of Leo and Gregory and contains lasting evidence of the times in which it was composed. "When the Goths, the Huns, and the Vandals were hovering over the moribund Roman Empire, like a flight of vultures preparing to pounce upon a dying camel in the desert as soon as the breath is out of his body, there was certainly some point, and there was likely to be some sincerity, in such a prayer" (Dean E. M. Goulburn, *The Collects of the Day*, 1883).

MEDITATION

This Collect concerns what is known as the First Use of the Law. In Reformation theology, stemming from the Reformers' intensive engagement with the Letters of St. Paul, the Law of God, meaning the Ten Commandments in particular, was understood to have two functions or uses.

The First Use of the Law (or *usus politicus* in Latin) is its function as the orderer or restrainer of chaos. Without the Commandments of God, the world would spin off its axis, galvanized by the negative energy of the death wish and libidinized aggression — which is modern parlance for sin. Human nature requires some restraint for the good of all. Without it, Thomas Malthus' picture of crowded, killing rats in a cage becomes actual.

The Second Use of the Law (or *usus theologicus*) is its function as the diagnoser of our human inability to perform the Law. This Second Use of the Law is a kind of mirror in which we see the way we ought to act and in which we are able at the same time to compare the way we do act. The comparison is odious. The Law's Second Use "stops every mouth" (Romans 3:19) — our desire to rationalize or justify our shortfalls. Therefore the Second Use becomes a "schoolmaster" (Galatians 3:23-25), leading us, by means of self-despair, to Christ.

The Collect for the Fifth Sunday after Trinity asks God to govern the world according to the Law's First Use. One result of godly order in the world is the Church's freedom to perform its leavening task "in all godly quietness."

The Prayer Book sees without question the need for ethical consensus, identified with the governance of God made concrete and universal in the Law of Moses. Without that Law, not only the world, but also the Christian Church is exposed to the primal viciousness of disordered human instinctual drives. We need the Law's First Use!

The Sixth Sunday after Trinity

THE COLLECT

od, which hast prepared to them that love thee such good things as pass all man's understanding; Pour into our hearts such love toward thee, that we loving thee in all things, may obtain thy promises, which exceed all that we can desire; through Christ our Lord.

HISTORY

While this is taken from the Gelasian Sacramentary via the Gregorian, the inspiration is clearly I Corinthians 2:9, itself a free quotation of Isaiah 64:4. Our love towards God is itself a gift from God.

Robert Browning's beautiful lines placed on the lips of the Savior:

"O heart I made, a heart beats here!
Face, my hands fashioned, see it in myself!
Thou hast no power nor mayst conceive of mine,
But love I gave thee, with myself to love,
And thou must love me who have died for thee!"

"An Epistle" (1855)

MEDITATION

This prayer, for the Sixth Sunday after Trinity, is as much loved as the Collect for the Fourth Sunday. Its focus is love.

The expression "God is Love" (I John 4:8) is a safe summary of the Christian faith. It hangs over the pulpit of the oldest free-church (i.e., non-Anglican) meetinghouse in England, Horningsham, near Longleat in Wiltshire. It is the Christian *précis* for the character of God. Although the phrase can be sentimentalized and become a Trojan Horse for any number of forced constructions "added of men," it is nevertheless a phrase which we hold to be true altogether and without condition because of Jesus Christ.

Note the order of ideas in this Collect. "Pour into our hearts such love towards thee." We do not or cannot love God without His help. That is because the human being fashions counterfeit gods continually. The true God Himself, the God of the First Commandment, can be construed also as wrath and destruction, hurricane and straight-line winds. So the prayer asks God to give us love for Him!

Without the love having shone in the face of Jesus Christ (II Corinthians 4:6), we would be kidding ourselves to love God without keeping our fingers crossed. The result of this given love is that we come to love God *in all things.* Here is the Augustinian and Reformed insight: God is active in all things, the bad (from our perspective) as well as the good. He is to be loved in all circumstances. This suggests a very deep level of acceptance. "Who is sufficient for these things?" (II Corinthians 2:16)

But the fruit of loving God in all things is, according to the prayer, the obtaining of the promises. And the promises are so good, that they "exceed all that we can desire." God is therefore not only Love, and to be loved; but He is good. The Collect is unconditional. It leaves no room for human bargaining, exemptions, or intellectual escape clauses. His love surpasses "*all* man's understanding," causes us to love Him "in *all* things," and results in (more than) "*all* that we can desire." This is the pummelling clarity of Prayer Book religion.

The Seventh Sunday after Trinity

THE COLLECT

ord of all power and might, which art the author and giver of all good things; graft in our hearts the love of thy name, increase in us true religion, nourish us with all goodness, and of thy great mercy keep us in the same; through Jesus Christ our Lord.

HISTORY

Gelasius began this Collect with the invocation "O Lord of Hosts," a phrase familiar to us in the Old Testament and in the *Te Deum*, "Lord God of Sabaoth."

Cranmer's translation of the acknowledgment phrase recalls James 1:17.

MEDITATION

There are great verbs in this prayer, grand askings: "graft," "increase," "nourish," and "keep." As always in the Prayer Book Collects, we are enjoined to ask God to do for us what we cannot do for ourselves. The prayer would mean nothing if we could self-graft love for God, if we could increase true religion by our own devices. The assumption is that left to ourselves we increase only in false religion, by which the Reformers meant some form of idolatry. The prayer would mean nothing if we could feed ourselves with self-engendered (thus illusory) goodness, and if we could keep ourselves from the wrong by means of natural willpower. The Collect's four verbs display the potency of God at the expense of the creature's impotence.

One of the four petitions requires particular explanation. What is "true religion," for which we are asking the increase? And not just true religion abstractly, but true religion in us? What is personal religion that is also true? And of what does false religion consist?

We know how the Reformers would have answered that. True religion accepts the full diagnosis of the psychogenetic defect known as sin. True religion casts all humanity's hope for release from the original universal defect on Christ, His sacrifice, and His resurrection. True religion looks to the Bible, and nothing beyond the Bible, for the Word from God about Christ. True religion results in and is the cause of the works of love, known classically as love of neighbor.

The Reformers understood any representation of Christianity that is untrue to any one of these four elements as a harming, pastorally cruel phenomenon to be resisted and opposed. False religion disappoints, causes outrageous reactions (especially within adolescents), fails to heal and give hope to lost people, and in a thousand ways maps out the way to God such that a person ends up either in the "slough of despond" (i.e., depression) or on a titanic pinnacle of earthborn self-righteousness. False religion, so asserts this Collect for Trinity VII, helps no one. True religion, on the other hand, is the great enabler of humane goodness.

The Eighth Sunday after Trinity

THE COLLECT

God, whose providence is never deceived, we humbly beseech thee that thou wilt put away from us all hurtful things, and give those things which be profitable for us; through Jesus Christ our Lord.

HISTORY

The Reformers gave the address and acknowledgment of this Gelasian Collect a rather odd translation from the Latin *cuius providentia in sui dispositione non fallitur* ("O God, whose providence is never failing in ordering that which is its own"). The 1662 revisers improved the translation to contain not only the thought that God in His Providence foresees everything, but also that He actually controls all things. He is never taken by surprise *and* He is in ultimate control.

MEDITATION

There is an arresting phrase at the start of the Collect. It brings you up short: "God, whose providence is never deceived."

The idea is that the purposes of God in the world, in our lives, and in every circumstance we can possibly imagine, cannot be turned aside. In particular — and this is the strange part to modern ears — the purposes of God cannot be turned aside by the devil's contrary voice or temptation. The picture is of God's good plan incapable of being sabotaged or subterfuged. We can call here upon the story of Christ's temptation in the wilderness. He was undeterred from His messianic purpose, to which a gallows was attached, by the blandishing "better ideas" of Satan.

We can be deceived. The fact that "you can fool some of the people all of the time" and "all of the people some of the time" is proof that no human being is invulnerable to deception. God is the great exception, in the same sense that Christ alone was without sin (Article XV). This being the case, we can trust the shape our lives are taking. The plan or big picture will not be derailed, even by the heaviest-breathing seduction.

Thus the Collect concludes with the confidence that God shall only present us with what is finally "profitable for us." This is as high a doctrine of Providence as you can get and puts the whole responsibility for the ultimate destiny of persons on the stronger-than-Promethean shoulders of the God made historic in the Friend of Sinners.

The Ninth Sunday after Trinity

THE COLLECT

rant to us Lord we beseech thee, the spirit to think and do always such things as be rightful; that we, which cannot be without thee, may by thee be able to live according to thy will; through Jesus Christ our Lord.

HISTORY

Massey Shepherd says of this Collect that "it expresses as succinctly as possible the whole doctrine of grace." Archbishop Cranmer tightly translated the Latin of this Leonine Collect (taken over by the Gelasian Sacramentary) *sine te esse,* "which cannot be (i.e., exist)." The revisers of 1662 changed this strong phrase to "we, who cannot do anything that is good without thee," thus weakening the 1549 Collect and changing the emphasis to prevenient grace.

MEDITATION

We are offered a curious phrase here describing the human condition: ". . . that we, which cannot be without thee."

One thinks of the passage in Romans 2, where St. Paul observes the universality of conscience as the primary human contact point with God. One does not have to be part of an elect nation to have converse with God. Whether He be named or recognized as God or not, He is relating everywhere and always to all humanity at the flash point of "the law written on the heart" (2:15).

The human race is never without God. God is driving, pushing, impelling towards the goal, working out His purpose in every situation, such that "we . . . cannot be without thee." Every situation and relationship has a third party. Or if one is alone, a second party, a witness. We are ever walking in His sight.

This is, as was said before in relation to earlier collects, both a terrible fact and a joy-conferring one. It is a terrible fact, because no one can elude God. Not Dorian Gray. Not Dr. Edward Jekyll. Not Mengele nor Stalin, even. Not you and I in our flights from accusation.

It is a joy-conferring fact, because it understands God to be there, right there, in the fiery furnace, the "fourth man" together with Shadrach, Meshach, and Abednego. They emerged with not one hair of their heads singed (Daniel 3:27). We can never be without God.

The Tenth Sunday after Trinity

THE COLLECT

Let thy merciful ears, O Lord, be open to the prayers of thy humble servants; and that they may obtain their petitions, make them to ask such things as shall please thee; through Jesus Christ our Lord.

HISTORY

This Collect is from the Gelasian Sacramentary, although a similar one appears in the Leonine. It consists of a twofold petition: that God may hear our prayer and that we may be led to ask according to His will (Romans 8:26-27).

MEDITATION

An important insight concerning prayer exists at the heart of this petition. But the insight is a hard saying.

God is implored to "make (us) to ask such things as shall please (Him), that (we) may obtain our petitions." In other words, our answer will depend on whether our prayer pleases God in the first place. It looks at first as if we need to know what God is thinking in order to know what sort of request He likes. Then ask it. Having been "consulted" beforehand, He will be glad to say yes.

This sounds like the student who, when asked a question by the professor, thinks to himself, "What does she want to hear?" Or you are facing an interview committee for a coveted position, and you ask yourself constantly, what do they want me to say? Or just as important, what do they want me not to say?

Can prayer be dishonest in such circular fashion? Does the nature of request hinge merely on the Granter's being apple-polished?

The answer has got to be no! Our relation with God is an absolutely open and frank "exchange of views," which hinges on the unconditional honesty of the creature before the Creator. So what is this all about?

It is about praying according to the Word of God and not contrary to it. On more than one occasion, this writer has heard the outpourings of a sincere Christian who is praying for God to give him something that the Word expressly denies. For example, someone asks God to give him or her a new wife or husband other than the one who already exists. Sometimes the one praying has a specific third party in mind! Or a person longs to be living an entirely different life, virtually in a different body and mind, than the life he or she is able to live. But God has given what He has given. Do not call unclean what God has called clean (Acts 10:15) and vice-versa!

This Collect invites us to pray for those changes and transformations in our lives that accord with righteousness, which we see explicit both in the Law (i.e., the Ten Commandments) and the Gospel (i.e., the life of Christ Jesus). Believe me, that gives us plenty of scope for our prayers!

The Eleventh Sunday after Trinity

THE COLLECT

od, which declarest thy almighty power, most chiefly in showing mercy and pity; Give unto us abundantly thy grace, that we, running to thy promises, may be made partakers of thy heavenly treasures; through Jesus Christ our Lord.

HISTORY

Thomas Cranmer's faithful translation of this Gelasian Collect was drastically altered by the revisers of 1662. Adding the phrase "that we, running the way of thy commandments, may obtain thy gracious promises . . ." makes the "heavenly treasures" ones which we can earn by obedience (the Law) rather than the true gift of God.

The Collect is closely linked to the Gospel for this day (St. Luke 9:15), the Parable of the Pharisee and the Publican, in which we see God's willingness to show mercy when He is approached with penitence and humility.

MEDITATION

The prayer discloses an insight concerning God's character which is of great importance. God is said here to declare His almighty power *most chiefly* in showing mercy and pity.

This gets to the heart of the Gospel question. It is a question to which our blessed Reformers gave their absolute all (and sometimes their bodies to be burned) in seeking to hear the answer: Is God primarily wrathful or is He primarily gracious (i.e., merciful)? More precisely, is God going to estimate me according to my deservings (Heaven forbid, at least if I am honest!) or according to some other standard of undeserved compassion? What, at the end of the day — at the end of my days — is God like?

This prayer makes the unambiguous and quite un-complex assertion that God demonstrates power primarily in pity. This is too much for my "natural man." Yet I ache for it through every fibre.

In an age when power and the acquisition (and abuse) of it is understood as *the* motivating force in human affairs — and every age, in fact, has marched somewhat to that devilish tune — this prayer stands in mighty contrast. It asserts a breathtaking alternative. God shows His power not chiefly in earthquake, fire, and flood, nor in the starry sky and earth beneath, nor in signs and wonders; but in pity.

In a terrifying movie by Abel Ferrara and Nicholas St. John entitled *The Funeral* (1996), a youth who has murdered a man is about to be executed in revenge by the man's brother. The youth pleads, "Don't do this. You have a chance to do something good, and that's better than justice." The executor is not God, however. The brother's "power" is declared in retribution.

That is not the God of the Collects, who is the God of the Scriptures. Our God is most powerful in His great moment: the forgiveness of our sins.

The Twelfth Sunday after Trinity

THE COLLECT

Almighty and everlasting God, which art always more ready to hear than we to pray, and art wont to give more than either we desire or deserve; Pour down upon us the abundance of thy mercy; forgiving us those things whereof our conscience is afraid, and giving unto us that that our prayer dare not presume to ask, through Jesus Christ our Lord.

HISTORY

Taken from the Sacramentary of Leo and revised by Gelasius, this prayer was altered in 1662. The 1549 wording is perhaps less smooth, but more faithful to the Latin. Bishop Cosin added, "and giving us those good things which we are not worthy to ask, but through the merits and mediation of Jesus Christ, thy Son, our Lord." The thought of our own just deserts is balanced by the merits of the Redeemer.

MEDITATION

This Collect is a treasure chest, truly overflowing, of uplifting insights drawn from our religion:

- God is more ready to hear us than we are to pray. We pray too little, too timorously, and too pallidly. We seldom pray for what we really need and while we are unceasingly preoccupied with our perceived needs, we simply pray too seldom! God is a listening ear, waiting for communications which too infrequently arrive. God is the more active dialogue-partner in the "I-Thou" conversation.

- God wills to give us more than we want and certainly more than we deserve. Can we for one second comprehend this? God does not work on the principle of distributive justice, i.e., "we get what we deserve." On the one hand, He wants to do more for us, in our impoverished frangibility, than we can conceive. On the other hand, He wants to do good to us rather than judge us according to our deservings. If He gave us what we deserve, who could stand? His grace is neither Aristotelian and distributive, nor quixotic and mercurial. He blesses — with abundance — and does not curse.

- We ask Him to forgive us the things that weigh on our conscience and cause us to fear to look Him in the eye. Even what seems to us, humanly speaking, unforgivable, can be forgiven by God. The reach of His mercy is further than our insight at its most layered and Freudian.

- We ask Him to give us what we cannot even imagine asking Him to give us. Again the Collect presents the overwhelming idea that God is able and desires to give us things that we cannot fathom even suggesting: such as change within an unchanging character fault, love when we have long given up hope of it, opportunity which we have stopped even seeking, and open doors when every door has slammed shut.

The Thirteenth Sunday after Trinity

THE COLLECT

lmighty and merciful God, of whose only gift it cometh that thy faithful people do unto thee true and laudable service; grant we beseech thee, that we may so run to thy heavenly promises, that we fail not finally to attain the same; through Jesus Christ our Lord.

HISTORY

Another ancient Collect (found in both the Leonine and Gelasian Sacramentaries) to which Archbishop Cranmer added the word "only." This prayer could be entitled "Basic Christianity." Our ability to give God laudable (i.e., praiseworthy) service is entirely dependent upon His grace — at every step of our Christian life. The revisers of 1662 altered the ending so forcefully that it changed the meaning.

MEDITATION

What does a promise mean to you? If someone promises that he or she will look after your child when you are gone, no matter what, does their promise give you the peace of mind you require? If someone promises something to me, I want the promise with all my heart to signal an absolute commitment on the part of the person to follow through!

A perfect if sentimental picture of a promise kept is an outlaw's word to a mother who had just given birth in a deserted covered wagon abandoned in the middle of a waterless desert. In *Three Godfathers* (1948), a John Ford Western, the John Wayne character, uncouth yet faithful, looks after the baby to the bitter (yet triumphal) end. He repeats constantly to himself, almost like an incantation, "I'm not going to break my promise to a dying woman!"

We could also remember the song and musical, *Promises! Promises!* We have seen enough promises broken, to the living as well as to the dead, to us even. The strength of a promise seems to have to depend on the trustworthiness of the one making the promise. And even then, people being human, we can be let down. The Cheyenne chiefs confronted Carl Schurz, Lincoln's old friend, with evidence of numberless promises broken by the U.S. government. Fortunately, Schurz made good! (He was later memorialized for his goodness by the city of New York. Thus we have Carl Schurz Park on the Upper East Side.)

The Scripture, and this Collect, invite us to run to the promises of God. This means to seize them and take to them; to move towards them enthusiastically without hanging back. They are of rock because of the Giver. When we run to the Giver of the astonishing promises of God to declare mercy to the pitiable and needy, the victims and victimizers of the world, we receive the Gift, which is the Holy Spirit with us. Trusting the promises of God is to "attain the same," for the fruit of such trust is serenity and peace.

The Fourteenth Sunday after Trinity

THE COLLECT

Almighty and everlasting God, give unto us the increase of faith, hope, and charity; and that we may obtain that which thou dost promise; make us to love that which thou dost command, through Jesus Christ our Lord.

HISTORY

Found in the earliest of the Sacramentaries, this Collect refers to I Corinthians 13. The first part of the Collect is closely connected with the second. Faith and hope permit us access to God's heavenly promises. Charity enables us to love that which He commands.

MEDITATION

Rarely has the logic of the Gospel been more succinctly stated than in this Collect. The logic of the Gospel is stated in the second and final petition: ". . . make us to love that which thou dost command."

The Petition is for the "I want" to cohere with the "I ought." As we have seen time after time in the Collects, the Law (i.e., "Thou shalt/shalt not") does not precede moral improvement (i.e., love of neighbor). In other words, doing good does not make one become good. Rather, love creates a person who desires to do good.

Law does not create Love. Love creates Law, or rather, Law-abidingness. The Collect asks God to make us people who wish and aspire to do, from the heart, what God has already commanded us to do.

The principle is foreshadowed in Romans 6:17: "Thanks be to God, that you who were once slaves of sin have become obedient from the heart to the standard of teaching to which you were committed." You have been set free, through the "love of God shed abroad in our hearts" (Romans 5:5), from the constraint of self-serving to the freedom of serving the other.

This exact dynamic, of Love preceding Law, is held up in one of the hymns composed by William Cowper (1731-1800) for the Olney hymnbook. It is entitled "Love Constraining to Obedience." Note this stanza which runs parallel to the Cranmer Collect:

> To see the law by Christ fulfilled,
>   And hear His pardoning voice,
> Changes a slave into a child,
>   And duty into choice.

The Fifteenth Sunday after Trinity

THE COLLECT

K eep we beseech thee, O Lord, thy church with thy perpetual mercy: and because the frailty of man without thee, cannot but fall: Keep us ever by thy help, and lead us to all things profitable to our salvation; through Jesus Christ our Lord.

HISTORY

The Gelasian Sacramentary provided this Collect for our Reformers who translated it into English, strangely omitting the phrase which follows "keep us ever by thy help." That phrase, *from all things hurtful,* was restored by the revisers of 1662.

MEDITATION

"All things profitable to our salvation": of what do these consist? We are told in I Corinthians 13 that we can do everything in the world that has the appearance of sacrifice, but if it is without love, it "profiteth us nothing" (v. 3).

The things that profit us in this particularly Christian sense will be characterized by love, in which what-can-this-do-for-me will play less and less a part. Anything built on self-involvement and self-preoccupation contributes nothing to our salvation, which is our enduring relation to God. On the other hand, anything characterized by outward-seeking love enriches the saved self.

Look for a moment at your interests or hobbies. You could draw a line between those avocations you have which feed withdrawal from love, and those avocations which restore you, such that communicativeness and extension of the self are the fruit. Ask yourself which of your interests, from tennis to cable TV to woodworking to biking to gardening to the movies to travel to gastronomy, are profitable, even from a purely human point of view.

It is possible that you have chosen well in your recreation and outside interests. It is also possible that you have chosen poorly. Your "hobby" could serve only the misunderstood cause of an escapism that isolates you (more and more), cuts you off from the ones you love, and ultimately profits neither you, nor the ones around you, nor in fact your relationship with God.

Take a look at your interests, the particular ones you daydream about when everyday living hits fever pitch. Are they profitable or are they hurtful? Lead us, O Lord, to all things profitable to our salvation.

The Sixteenth Sunday after Trinity

THE COLLECT

ord, we beseech thee, let thy continual pity cleanse and defend thy congregation; and, because it cannot continue in safety without thy succor, preserve it evermore by thy help and goodness; through Jesus Christ our Lord.

HISTORY

In translating another Gelasian Collect, Archbishop Cranmer rendered *ecclesiam* as "congregation." The 1662 revisers substituted "Church" in reaction to the Puritan use of the former term. "Church" is also used in the Scottish Prayer Book of 1637.

MEDITATION

Let thy congregation escape tribulation:
Thy Name be ever praised! O Lord, make us free!

(The Hymnal 1982, No. 433)

The hymn we sing on Thanksgiving Day, "We Gather Together," is a perfect paraphrase of the Collect's first Petition: "Let thy continual pity cleanse and defend thy congregation." The hymn was written, anonymously, around 1625 to celebrate the accession of Frederick Henry, Prince of Orange, to the leadership of the United Provinces of Holland. The Prince of Orange was the defender of the Reformed Church's liberties against Spain. The hymn embodies the same prayer for Church and Nation which Cranmer included here seventy-five years earlier. In Cranmer's mind, the Collect understands the Church in its Gospel identity as enduringly fragile: ". . . it cannot continue in safety without thy succor." So he prays that the congregation of Christ would be cleansed, defended, and preserved.

The point to underline for us is the link between God's pity and God's cleansing. People sometimes say, "I don't want your pity. That's the last thing I need." This is "pity" understood as a superior's resented sympathy, peering down from on high. It smarts one's pride.

"Pity" here, in the Collect for Trinity XVI, refers to God's compassion, His disposition and temperament of mercy that is continual, unchanging. The idea is that this compassion has the potency to cleanse. We can liken it to that power of tenderly affected empathy for us in our need that is able to reduce us to tears. The empathy of another who truly loves me moves me. Christ's pity on the Syrophoenician woman, the man born blind, pathetic Zacchaeus, Mary Magdalene, Bartimaeus at Jericho, me and you: This can touch us where we live. Being moved to tears and the emotional encounter of being loved in our real state cleanses us. Let His continual pity cleanse and defend us evermore.

The Seventeenth Sunday after Trinity

THE COLLECT

ord we pray thee that thy grace may always prevent and follow us, and make us continually to be given to all good works through Jesus Christ our Lord.

HISTORY

This Collect from the Sacramentary of Gregory is a prayer for prevenient and cooperating grace, as in the Collect for Easter Day. Its Gregorian origin interrupts the Gelasian sequence that began on the Sixth Sunday after Trinity.

The word Archbishop Cranmer translated as "continually" is the Latin *iugiter* — like an everflowing stream. Grace is not occasional, it

> Ever flows our thirst to assuage;
> Grace which like the Lord the giver,
> Never fails from age to age.

MEDITATION

Understanding this Collect turns on the simple fact that the verb "prevent" in the older English means "precede" in modern English. The prayer asks God to send His grace (i.e., unmerited favor) before us, in front of us as we travel our road, as well as behind us. It is the "pillar of cloud by day and the pillar of fire by night" (Exodus 13:21).

The same idea is expressed in the famous hymn *St. Patrick's Breastplate:*

Christ be with me, Christ within me,
Christ behind me, Christ before me,
Christ beside me, Christ to win me,
Christ to comfort and restore me.

Without God having already gone before us, we would, as human beings in our own strength, face impossible odds. We have heard this insight repeatedly in the Collects. Without Him we are not up to what Mr. Murdstone in *David Copperfield* termed so chillingly the "battle of life." What lies ahead of us, humanly speaking, is too uncertain, too hostile, too large, too callous, too cold, too hard, too impossible. The Collects emphasize the frailty of our case and the dangers in which we are perpetually set, circling the human being like sharks and vultures. If He were not going before us, not to mention covering our flanks, we would, in general, within ourselves, simply freeze.

This writer was once in a dark mood of bitter complaint. Having had a glorious and restful sabbatical overseas, he said offhandedly to someone, even bitterly: "I cannot face going back. It is too much and too hard." My friend listened, then chided me, "Wait a minute. Do you really think that the same Christ you adore here will not also be waiting for you *there* as you walk down the runway?" The prevenient grace of God was the speaker's point of reference. His words proved true.

The Eighteenth Sunday after Trinity

THE COLLECT

ord we beseech thee, grant thy people grace to avoid the infections of the Devil, and with pure heart and mind to follow thee the only God; through Jesus Christ our Lord.

HISTORY

This Gelasian Collect originally was appointed for the Sunday prior to the autumn Ember Days (times of penitence and ordination). The revisers of 1662 changed Cranmer's translation to read "to withstand the temptation of the world, the flesh, and the devil." It is not possible always to avoid temptation which may lie in our path, but we can withstand it by God's grace. The alteration thus links this Collect to the traditional Prayer Book baptismal vows.

MEDITATION

They asked the learned provost of Eton College and celebrated writer of supernatural fiction, M. R. James (1862-1936), what the secret was of writing a good mystery. He said that everything depends on the mechanism of the mystery. What exactly has happened that now needs to be found out? The writer needs to work back from whatever it is that has been covered up.

The same principle applies to interpreting the Collects of 1549. What is the governing idea of the prayer? Better, what is the Collect asking? Everything else, the address, the acknowledgment, the aspiration, the very meaning itself, hinge on the *petition*.

In the Collect for the Eighteenth Sunday after Trinity, the "infections of the Devil" are to be avoided and a "pure heart and mind" to be conferred. The prayer turns on the contrast between infection and purity. The Devil seeks to make us sick, thereby making us also contagious. The Word of God cleanses us.

The picture is of an actual foe, a personal power, striving to infect the Christian through the entry point of his weakness. Once the sickness, being bitterness, shame, resentment, comparison, unmourned loss, and the like, has been transmitted, mainly through the tempting voice of despair, it spreads. The "wiles" of the Devil (Ephesians 6:11) are transmitted, or carried from person to person, in conversation as well as in the tone and tenor of one's spirit and behavior. Corruption contaminates.

Avoidance is a better way, not baiting the evil impulse or trying to withstand it, but giving it (him!) a wide berth. The uninfected human being is a pure human being. And purity issues in following God. Following God issues from purity.

Pray the Collect until you have laid hold of the mechanism. In this case it is purity, the antithesis of infection. Then don't let go of this gold. The consequence will be that you shall be following God.

The Nineteenth Sunday after Trinity

THE COLLECT

God, for as much as without thee, we are not able to please thee; Grant that the working of thy mercy may in all things direct and rule our hearts; through Jesus Christ our Lord.

HISTORY

The original from the Gelasian Sacramentary ran "let the working of thy mercy direct our hearts, for without thee we are not able to please thee."

Cranmer reversed the order so that the acknowledgment of our inability comes first, as experientially it must. He also added "and rule" after "direct," for we do not need more guidance but we do need the power to carry out His will.

MEDITATION

A famous opening: "O God, for as much as without thee, we are not able to please thee." It is a picture of God that is somewhat circular. He is the One who by definition can be pleased only by someone like Himself, that is, like must commune with like.

This is an old concept from philosophy: God is that than which there can be no higher or better or purer, for He can "by no means behold iniquity" (Habakkuk 1:13). He can commune alone with that which is like Him, i.e., perfect. Hence His creatures require His aid in order to approach Him, let alone live in harmony with Him. Yes, the Collect opens famously — and threateningly.

But the mechanism of the prayer lies elsewhere than in the opening. The mechanism lies in the asking for the operation of God's mercy to direct and rule. This is unusual. The Collect might have implored God's *authority* or God's *command* or God's irresistible *constraint* to govern our hearts. Discretion and rule, after all, imply control. But no! We call here on God's *mercy,* His compassion and unmerited favor, to sway us. Grace is to direct us.

This is the Gospel pearl in the Collect for Trinity XIX. Love for the ungodly (Romans 5:6, 8) moves the ungodly. Mercy breaks my heart. It makes me become merciful. We know this from friendship, marriage, parenthood. We know this from the crises of our life. We know this from the God who loved the world. We count on it here.

The Twentieth Sunday after Trinity

THE COLLECT

Almighty and merciful God, of thy bountiful goodness, keep us from all things that may hurt us; that we, being ready both in body and soul, may with free hearts accomplish those things that thou wouldest have done; through Jesus Christ our Lord.

HISTORY

Although originally from the Gelasian Sacramentary, this Collect has undergone a great deal of "remodeling" over the years. Cranmer substituted the phrase "of thy bountiful goodness" for the Latin *propitiatus* (which means "being propitiated") because of the association with the false Roman doctrine of the propitiatory nature of the Mass (Article XXXI).

The archbishop also substituted "those things that thou wouldest have done" for "the things that are thine," although this change obscures the contrast between "things that may hurt us" in the first part of the Collect and the good things that belong to God.

This Collect is appointed for the Confirmation service in the South African Prayer Book.

MEDITATION

The mainspring for this prayer is the petition to be enabled to do what God wants us to do. Conversely, the petition is for us not to do what God wants us not to do.

The issue or question, however, is *how*. How can we possibly aspire to do, let alone actually do, the right thing? Someone comes to the rector for counselling. The rector asks, "What do you really want?" The person who has come for help replies, "I want to do the right thing." But the right thing may feel like the impossible thing, even the inconceivable thing. It may be a case of the hard right against the easy wrong. How can we hope to do it?

The key phrase in the Collect is this: "with free hearts," "that we may *with free hearts* accomplish. . . ." Our doing right depends again — and this is the secret of the Prayer Book Collects — on a freedom that results from confident belovedness. Doing right is not the result of command. It does not issue from control. It is not a question of authority, headship, patriarchy, or submission. So far the Collect accords with the modern spirit of freedom. The deeper or universal accord, however, is with the New Testament: "Where the Spirit of the Lord is, there is liberty" (II Corinthians 3:17; St. John 8:31-32). Put precisely, "God has not given us a spirit of fear, but of power, of love and of a sound mind" (II Timothy 1:7).

Freedom, then, is the freedom which comes from God. The consequence of such freedom is, in the proper sense, free love, love without constraint, love not forced or pressured or bargained for. We have found and we know that such love is the fulcrum that moves the world.

The Twenty-First Sunday after Trinity

THE COLLECT

rant we beseech thee, merciful Lord, to thy faithful people pardon and peace, that they may be cleansed from all their sins, and serve thee with a quiet mind. Through Jesus Christ our Lord.

HISTORY

This is the last of the Collects taken from the Gelasian Sacramentary. Cranmer changed the original "indulgence" to "pardon" because of the medieval abuse associated with the prior term.

In Gelasius' time the *Pax Romana* which had made the world secure was breaking up, hence the plea for the peace "which passeth all human understanding" (Philippians 4:7) as that which alone can endure the trials and unrest of the world.

This Collect is sometimes used in the Church of England to replace the Absolution in Morning and Evening Prayer when those services are conducted by a lay reader.

110

MEDITATION

Do you ever see yourself as a "stormy petrel" or a "squeaky wheel," an angular person or an edgy person, or a plain worried, anxious person? Chances are you do not. But others may. You can certainly answer the question, do you possess a quiet or peaceful mind? You alone know the answer to that.

The Collect asks for pardon and peace, with the incomparable result of "a quiet mind." Freedom from the heavy dead hand of the past produces the opposite of anxiety. It produces tranquillity, which in this case means no fear. A memorable example of such a state of inward tranquillity is observed towards the beginning of Victor Hugo's novel *Les Miserables.* The hero, and culprit, Jean Valjean, is robbing the house of his benefactor, Monsieur Bienvenu, who is a provincial bishop. As Valjean creeps through the bishop's bedroom towards the dining room of the house, where the silver is, he cannot avoid glancing at the bishop's sleeping face. Valjean is transfixed by what he sees:

> Jean Valjean advanced, carefully avoiding the furniture. At the far end of the room he could hear the even, quiet breathing of the sleeping bishop. . . .
>
> He was almost completely dressed in bed, because of the cold Basse-Alpes nights. His head was tilted back on the pillow in the unstudied attitude of sleep. His face was lit up with a vague expression of contentment, hope, and happiness. It was almost a radiance, a luminous transparency, for this heaven was within him: it was his conscience.
>
> Jean Valjean stood in the shadow, erect, motionless, terrified. He had never seen anything like it. The moral world has no spectacle more powerful than this: a troubled, restless conscience on the verge of committing a crime, contemplating the sleep of a just man.

That is the picture of a quiet mind.

The Twenty-Second Sunday after Trinity

THE COLLECT

Lord we beseech thee to keep thy household the church in continual godliness; that through thy protection it may be free from all adversities, and devoutly given to serve thee in good works, to the glory of thy name; through Jesus Christ our Lord.

HISTORY

In the original from the Gregorian Sacramentary, the expression "thy Church and household" represents the Latin *familia,* family. In a Roman household not only was the *familia* made up of relatives but also of master and servant — all dependent upon the *pater familias* who cared for all. The Collect is connected beautifully to the Gospel for the Day (St. Matthew 18:21ff.).

MEDITATION

This prayer is for the Church. It is relatively commonplace and says what we might expect it to say. It is as when the village parson in Agatha Christie's *Murder at the Vicarage* comes upon the squire's wife and her younger lover embracing, and moments afterward the lady rushes guiltily into the vicar's study and asks him, "What do you have to say, vicar?" He replies, almost helplessly, "Mrs. Protheroe, what do you *expect* me to say?"

So this Collect properly beseeches God for the godliness of the Church, its protection from threat and disaster, and its ministry of devout service. So far so good, and so fitting.

But there is a little more to it than that. The Church is the household of God (Ephesians 2:19). It is a family keeping company together. It is a family in operation, not in theory. "Household" suggests activity, support, unity yet with plurality, focus yet with variety; not oneness at the expense of manyness, nor manyness at the expense of oneness. Household suggests a clear direction yet with the necessary working on the part of all hands. We run parallel here with the somewhat more theological image of the Body of Christ.

We receive from the Collect, then, a vision of the Christian Church as a oneness in motion and the manyness required for the sustaining of such motion. There is nothing static here, nor obdurate.

The Twenty-Third Sunday after Trinity

THE COLLECT

God, our refuge and strength, which art the author of all godliness, be ready to hear the devout prayers of thy church; and grant that those things which we ask faithfully we may obtain effectually; through Jesus Christ our Lord.

HISTORY

Taken from the Gregorian Sacramentary, the Collect is based on the familiar words of Psalm 46, "God is our refuge and strength." There is a play here on the Latin *pietatis* (of godliness) and *piis* (devout prayers), which Stephens-Hodge notes may be rendered "thou author of devotion, hear our devoted prayer."

MEDITATION

The energizing heart of what is asked here is the receiving in fact of that which is prayed for in hope.

It is one thing to implore God for sanctuary or refuge, and in the sincerest manner. It is another thing to "obtain (it) effectually." Note the obtaining that is petitioned in the Collect and also the obtaining in such manner that it works — effectually.

Christ said in St. Matthew's Gospel that we can expect to receive what we pray for in the trust that it will be done (21:21-22). It is easy to flag in one's confidence concerning that particular promise. Nevertheless, faithful prayer takes place quite often. It is when we turn a burden over to God and feel our own burden become lighter, even lighter in seconds.

Asking faithfully is in itself an answer. It produces tangible peace of mind. It may issue also in results that others can see. A besetting circumstance can change. The point of the Collect is the relation between faith and effect. Giving over, which is faith, is connected to a consequence, which results in life.

This writer asked a sufferer, "When you pray about that particular thing, what happens?" "I always feel better," he answered. He added, "And I can take the next step."

Grant that what we ask for in hope we may obtain in fact.

The Twenty-Fourth Sunday after Trinity

THE COLLECT

Lord we beseech thee, absolve thy people from their offences, that through thy bountiful goodness we may be delivered from the bands of all those sins, which by our frailty we have committed: Grant this, &c.

HISTORY

A Collect found both in the Leonine and Gregorian Sacramentaries, its original use was on the Sunday prior to autumn ordinations (perhaps a link with the priestly authority of absolution). Its transference by our Reformers to the penultimate Sunday of the Christian year is curiously appropriate. As the year closes, we are conscious of the things we have done and the things we have left undone. But our sins, if confessed, need hold no terror for us. We have been "delivered from the bands of those sins, which by our frailty we have committed." Blessed assurance!

MEDITATION

"I am not asking your acceptance of what I have done. I am asking your forgiveness." An awesome request! "Please do not say that what I have done is nothing. Rather, absolve me."

This prayer has two points of view, that of victim and that of victimizer. But the latter looms larger than the former. The petition is for the forgiveness of offenses committed. This is the primary request. But the prayer goes on to see us sinners as victims also, victims of compulsion: ". . . the bands of all those sins which by our frailty we have committed." Sins bind us, yet we commit sins because we are frail.

The sequence of the human tragedy goes this way: Our frailty or need leaves us open to temptation. When we fall, we become as it were imprisoned. Each sin is another brick in the wall, or what Jacob Marley in *A Christmas Carol* described as the links of the chain we have wrought in life. The human condition is one of imprisonment, the prison being the compulsion which springs from our neediness. For release to be accomplished, forgiveness is needed. Thus the prayer asks God to do the one thing sufficient to break the bondage. Father, forgive!

In modern language, I am a victim first in time, the victim of my constraining weakness. I become thereby a victimizer, creating the chain of sins which I by the end of my life "have committed." These chainlinks are my offenses. Relief for my problem comes, first, not in recognizing the victimization which preceded my victimizing others, but first in receiving forgiveness for my sins. Absolution is the hammer blow that breaks the cycle. Then I can develop the compassion which understands both myself and others eking out a constricted life within the bands of sin.

The Good News, then, is for victimizers or sinners first, and for victims or those sinned against second. How do you read this? Does it bless the criminal first, through forgiveness, and only then proceed on to the victim? No and yes. What it does do is address in the sharpest possible manner the criminal, and in doing so observes the victim that lies beneath the surface of the culprit. Victimizer and victim coexist within every single human being.

No self-righteousness allowed!

The Twenty-Fifth Sunday after Trinity

THE COLLECT

tir up we beseech thee, O Lord, the wills of thy faithful people, that they, plenteously bringing forth the fruit of good
works, may of thee, be plenteously rewarded; through Jesus
Christ our Lord.

HISTORY

This Collect from the Gregorian Sacramentary is linked to the season
of Advent. Should there be more than twenty-five Sundays after
Trinity, Collects from the shortened Epiphany season may be used as
needed between Trinity XXIV and Trinity XXV, in order to insure
that this Collect is always used on "the Sunday next before Advent."
That title, from the Sarum Missal, was not used by Cranmer but was
restored in the American revision of 1892.

A popular name is "Stir Up Sunday" (Latin *excita*, stir up to
greater activity), a reference both to God's power and man's will. It
was also a reminder that it was time for members of the family to take
turns stirring the Christmas pudding in preparation for that feast.

MEDITATION

This famous Collect, with its striking opening imperative, "Stir up . . . , O Lord," conveys the Gospel message in a nutshell. It is a memorable summary of all that has gone before.

The will is incalculably strong. We know that. If you want or will to do something, it almost always gets done. We say of someone, not too charitably, there goes a person who does what she wants to do. Or, he always gets his way. Or, once your father set his cap on something, he always got it!

The will gets what it wills. The question is, what does your will will, or want? If your will is really free to choose, *what* is it free to choose? We observe that the will is free in that it can move mightily. But who or what sets its course? A part of your will can wish to go in one direction but be "outvoted" by stronger inner voices. "The good that I would do, I do not, and the evil that I would not, that I do" (Romans 7:15, 19). Is the will free to decide what it wants?

The will needs to be stirred. I need to be animated! Something needs to fire up my desire to act. I need inspiration.

God, here, is implored to give our wills inspiration. Once inspired, we shall bring forth "the fruit of good works." As we have seen all along the line, all actions have points of origin. In Christianity, action that is truly free has been relieved of constraint (i.e., binding anger, grievance, bitterness, etc.) by the prior love of Christ to "the ungodly" (Romans 5:6, 8). Stirred by the apprehension of being loved, the will brings forth the works of love. The consequence of such love that creates love is "plenteous reward."

This is the Gospel order: the love of Christ to needy sinners; the animating (or better, reanimating) effect of that love; the fruit of ethical loving which springs from the reanimated will; and the reward of that love-from-love, which is partial in the here and now and total in heaven.

Thus Thomas Cranmer's Gospel Collects of 1549.